High Yield, Small Space
ORGANIC GARDENING

T0357053

High Yield, Small Space
ORGANIC GARDENING

Practical Tips for Growing Your Own Food

Christy Wilhelmi
Owner of Gardenerd

High Yield, Small Space Organic Gardening

Managing Editor: Gretchen Bacon
Acquisitions Editor: Lauren Younker
Editor: Christa Oestreich
Designer: Mike Deppen
Indexer: Jay Kreider

ISBN 978-1-58011-611-4

Library of Congress Control Number: 2024944507

We are always looking for talented authors. To submit an idea, please send a brief inquiry to acquisitions@foxchapelpublishing.com.

Printed in China
First Printing

Creative Homeowner®, *www.creativehomeowner.com*, is an imprint of New Design Originals Corporation and distributed in North America by Fox Chapel Publishing Company, Inc., 800-457-9112, 903 Square Street, Mount Joy, PA 17552.

DEDICATION

FOR DAVID KING, A TRUE FRIEND AND GARDEN MASTER

ACKNOWLEDGMENTS

This book was first published as *Gardening for Geeks* in 2013. Now, more than a decade later, the information is still relevant and helpful to new and experienced gardeners alike. This book has the same valuable lessons and projects, just organized in a way that's easier to read and follow the projects.

The updated version of this book would never have happened were it not for Katie Elzer-Peters, who introduced me to Bud Sperry at Fox Chapel Publishing, and everyone at Fox Chapel, who gave new life to *Gardening for Geeks*. Special thanks to Andrew Cheeseman, for always encouraging the best in me, and to Jonathan Blank, who knows a thing or two about book publishing and willingly spent time sharing it with me—I cannot thank you enough.

I must draw particular attention to the garden geeks who have inspired my gardening exploits throughout the years (in no particular order): John Jeavons, the late Mel Bartholomew, the late Geoff Hamilton, Rosalind Creasy, Michael Pollan, David King, Jere Gettle, Louise Riotte, Barbara Kingsolver, and everyone at Ocean View Farms organic community garden. To those who helped clarify the material for this book, I appreciate the access you afforded me: Victoria Boudman of the Square Foot Gardening Foundation, Eben Fodor of SunWorks, Master Preserver Rose Wilde of Red Bread Bakery, irrigation wunderkind Russell Ackerman, and, again, John Jeavons of Ecology Action.

Last, but never least, I must thank my parents, Frank and Jo Wilhelmi, for being the engineer/carpenter and nurse/wonder-cook geeks who begat this geek.

CONTENTS

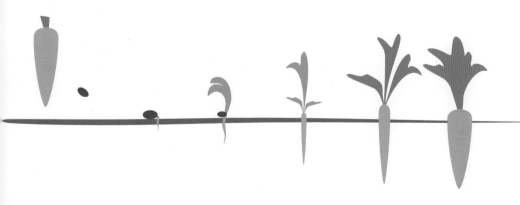

INTRODUCTION

What's It All About?

When garden nerds (or Gardenerds) get excited about a subject, they want to know everything. Gardening is an exciting topic—a vast world of soil biology, botany, and horticulture. It cross-pollinates with the insect world, meteorology, and nutrition. The more we learn about gardening, the more we realize there is to learn. It's a wonderfully addictive passion to have.

Do you want to know everything? This is a great place to start, but keep in mind that gardening knowledge doesn't arrive in a specific sequence. With the exception of the seasonal calendar or a planting schedule, gardening is not linear. It shifts each year, challenging us to figure out nature's next step. It tests our instincts as much as our knowledge, and, in the end, nature always wins. Most of the time, we benefit from nature's triumph, but just like Olympic athletes, gardeners experience both the thrill of victory and the agony of defeat.

This book is meant to be a gateway into all things cool about gardening. It gives you the basics to start designing and building the garden of your dreams. It also will lead you to bigger concepts to explore later, when you're ready. It delves into the science of how plants work, how soil lives, and how bugs help. Even

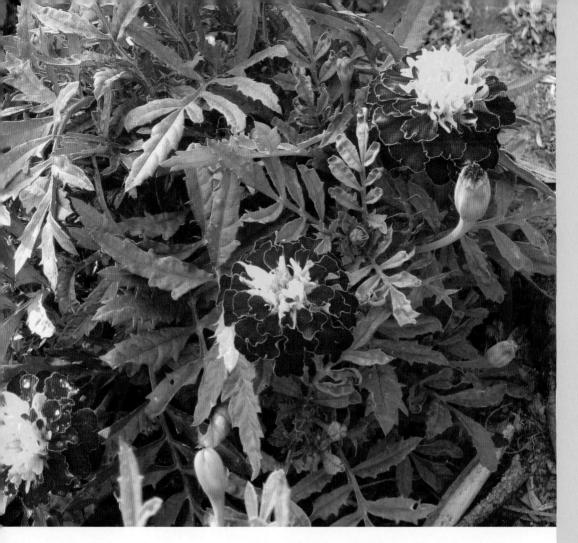

Marigolds serve multiple functions in the garden:
they offer beauty as well as pest control benefits.
Some types have pollen and nectar too.

though the book takes you step by step through the process, I encourage you to jump around. Early on, you'll notice references to Part 2's DIY section. If you can't wait, feel free to jump forward and read. Whatever floats your boat!

The information in this book is compiled from several classes I teach, with extra-bonus nerdy details that don't fit into the confines of the classroom. Students have been asking me to put it all down in one place. Well, here it is. Have at it. I hope you enjoy this journey into the science side of gardening. Put on your gloves, and let's get started.

Happy gardening!

PART 1: Gardening A–Z

Whether you are at the beginning of your gardening journey or well into the process, the information in Part 1 will help you get ready for the best gardening season of your life. Each chapter offers techniques and tips to improve your gardening space and to create the foundation of a successful, healthy, small-space garden. You may feel the impulse to hurry up and get growing, but take a breath, take a moment, and implement the lessons in this section. Later on, when you are harvesting baskets of produce from your small-space garden, you'll be glad you took the time to follow these steps.

From soil prep to raised beds, from planning to planting, Part 1 has all the guidance you need. You'll also find advice to help you figure out irrigation, water catchment, pest control, and what to do with the harvest (yum!). Get ready to grow big in your small space. Together, we can make the most of the garden we've got.

CHAPTER 1

Creating Your Garden Ecosystem

There are many things to consider when planning a garden. Location is everything, but not the only thing. Sure, it's important to make sure that your garden will get enough sun (a minimum of six hours per day), but let's talk about the other factors. Let's talk about your garden ecosystem. After all, your garden is a community of living things, and, for it to flourish, they will all have to get along together.

Wherever your garden is located, be it on a balcony, on a patio, or in a backyard, you will want to create an environment that supports your efforts. Your garden's ecosystem can provide shelter, windbreaks, and even pest-control assistance if you include a few key elements. From simple to more complex, the following components all play a role in that ecosystem.

A water source for pollinators and wildlife is part of your ecosystem.

Habitats

Established trees are an important part of your garden's ecosystem. Not only do they absorb carbon dioxide and release oxygen for a healthier planet, but they also provide a place for birds and insects to live. Ants and other insects crawl through the trees' bark, and birds take advantage of that traffic. Birds build nests and lay their young or visit on their way to higher latitudes. Then they scavenge your garden for food, and, in the process, they provide pest-management services for you, gobbling up bugs and worms.

You can help provide a reason for birds to congregate in your garden by hanging bird feeders and seed cakes. Birdhouses, made from gourds or wood, provide a habitat as well. Many gardeners grow sunflowers, which develop dinner-plate-sized seedheads, to attract birds. While it's true that these winged creatures will enjoy your sunflowers whether you want them to or not, the benefits of having birds in the garden generally outweigh the negative effects.

Bats

Bats, if you have them in your neck of the woods, help reduce the pest population by swooping through the sky at dusk like airborne vacuum cleaners, eating bugs in midflight. According to Bat Conservation International, bats consume "night-flying insects, including many of the most damaging agricultural pests . . . A single little brown bat can eat up to 1,000 mosquito-sized insects in a single hour."

Consider a bat house to attract this helpful animal to your garden.

Bats serve other purposes as well. Did you know that they are pollinators? As they drink nectar from flowers, they help pollinate many cacti and fruiting plants. As a bonus, they leave behind droppings called *guano*, which happens to be among the best fertilizers around. Bat droppings include 11%–16% nitrogen, 8%–12% phosphoric acid, and 2%–3% potash—all components of healthy soil. Guano can also serve as a composting starter and a fungicide.

If you are reluctant to welcome bats into your world, this is a good time to let go of creepy bat stereotypes. With bat populations in serious decline, they need all the help they can get. You can install a bat house on a wall under the eaves of a home, garage, or shed to encourage bats to take up residence. Bat houses are narrow boxes with even narrower compartments inside (about ¾" [2cm] deep) that allow bats a place of safe, dark shelter. In a study published in *The Bat House Researcher* in spring 2004, it was revealed that bats prefer larger bat houses (at least 20" [51cm] wide x 25" [64cm] high) that are painted and mounted on buildings rather than mounted on posts or trees. You can find several free plans for building your own bat house, along with tips for attracting bats, on the Bat Conservation International website, *batcon.org*.

Toads

Toads are another great addition, and pest consumer, for your garden. They consume slugs (yay!) and worms (such as nasty cutworms that mow down your kale plants before the seedlings ever reach harvesting size). Granted, toads don't inhabit every climate zone, but where there is moisture and shelter, they often make a home. Make a toad house out of a terra-cotta pot by chipping off a wedge of the upper rim of the pot. Turn the pot over, nestle it into a grassy corner, and *voilà!* You have a toad house with a little entryway. Provide a water source, like a fountain or shallow pond, and toads will find your garden very desirable.

Bees

Bees are critically important to our garden ecosystem. They are responsible for pollinating a huge percentage of crops, constituting one out of every three bites of food we eat. Without bees, we wouldn't have many of the fruits and vegetables we bring to the table. The presence of bees in your garden can boost yields by between 10 and 50 percent, according to independent studies on a variety of crops. Even crops that don't require bees in order to set fruit appear to benefit. Cheryl Miller of Sustainable Harvest

A honey bee rests on a beekeeper's arm.

International reported on coffee farmers in Honduras for The Rodale Institute, explaining that "coffee plants are capable of self-pollination, so for a long time researchers did not think insects made much difference to the crop. But studies show that when bees pollinate coffee plants, yields can increase by more than 50 percent."

Farmers hire beekeepers to bring hives to their fields, but urban beekeeping is gaining popularity with home gardeners. As colony collapse disorder (CCD) continues to decimate the world's bee population (theories about what causes it range from cell phones to mites to pesticides), gardeners are taking the fight into their own hands by setting up beehives as part of their ecosystems. Some place hives on their roofs, while others situate their hives in corners of their backyards, pointing toward walls to direct bees upward on a path away from humans. You can find instructions for how to build a swarm box to attract bees to your garden in Part 2.

To encourage bees and other beneficial insects, grow beneficial flowers. What the heck are those, you ask? Let's take a closer look.

> ### GARDENING TIP:
> # BE ONE WITH THE BEE
>
> **Bees only become aggressive if their hive is being threatened. Many gardeners enjoy tending their gardens while bees hover nearby. Bees come and go as they please, pollinating your vegetables and fruit trees, increasing yields, and leaving behind a legacy of bountiful harvests.**

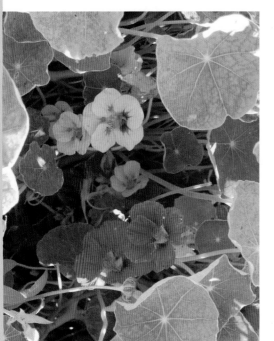

Beneficial Flowers and Their Friends

Some beneficial flowers attract pollinators, such as bees and wasps, to the garden. Other types of flowers attract insect predators, such as parasitic wasps (about the size of a gnat) and praying mantises. Still another type of flower works like a trap crop, excreting an odor that attracts pests to the plant instead of your valuable crops. Calendula or nasturtiums, for example, are reliable trap crops, because

Nasturtiums act as a trap crop to lure pests to their flowers instead of your veggies.

they have a strong scent, and it isn't uncommon to find them infested with aphids. Great! Leave those aphids right there. Now they aren't destroying your broccoli plants. With trap crops, you can isolate pests to one area of your garden and avoid using sprays to control their populations.

No More Pests?

Why not just wipe pests out altogether? Good question—and the answer is even better. If you eliminate pests completely, then the beneficial insects will have nothing to eat. Remember, your ecosystem is all about balance. Have the right balance of ingredients (in this case, pests versus beneficial insects), and your garden will achieve a balance all its own. You won't have to work as hard to keep pests under control, and you'll be able to enjoy more of your harvest in an unmolested state. We'll discuss specific plants to include in your ecosystem in Chapter 9 in the Good Bugs versus Bad Bugs section. For now, just know that planting flowers can be beneficial to your garden's health.

Calendula and hyacinth feed pollinators.

Where should you plant them? Just like trees, beneficial flowers function wonderfully as a hedge or border to your garden. Plant flowers around the perimeter to encourage insects to make a home there. Flowers can also be planted between crops to assist with pest control in planter beds. A combination of both scenarios will help ensure balance.

Garden Orientation

Get out your compass; it's time to determine the best orientation for your garden. If you live in the northern hemisphere, a south-facing garden is best (in the southern hemisphere, of course, the opposite is true). The sun rises in the east, and because the earth's axis is tilted, the sun travels across the sky from east to west at a southerly angle. Therefore, if your garden is situated so that it is exposed to that southerly arc of the sun's path, your garden will get the full-sun exposure—at least six hours per day—that is required to grow vegetables. Many times, situating a garden at the

A sundial watch and a compass ring can be handy, easy-to-carry garden tools.

northernmost point of the yard allows for the best southerly exposure. If your yard is shadowed by trees or tall buildings, the best location for a garden may indeed be your front yard. The open streets often allow for unobstructed full-sun gardening.

In the winter, the sun's arc is lower in the sky, so shadows from surrounding buildings or trees will be longer. Take this into account when planning out your location if you live in a climate where winter gardening is feasible. If the only space available gets sun in the summer but is in shadow in the winter, consider planting crops that do well in partial sunlight or shade during that time. Swiss chard, kale, strawberries, and many herbs will tolerate partial shade.

Another thing to consider when plotting out your planter beds or rows is their orientation. Again, full-sun exposure is the goal. If you lay out your beds or rows with the longest sides running east to west (yes, this is contrary to what some experts say), your plants will have equal access to that full southern exposure as the sun crosses the sky. For example, let's say you have a 4' x 8' (1.2 x 2.4m) raised bed. Orient the bed so that the long side, the 8' (2.4m) length, runs from east to west. Why does this really matter? The answer lies in the next part of planning your garden's orientation.

Plant Placement

Once your garden is laid out, you can start planning what plants go where. This may seem obvious, but it's a bit of a trick to ensure the best sun exposure for your plants. It's time to think about the vegetables you want to grow in terms of their height. For best results, place tall and trellised plants toward the north, and shorter or trailing plants to the south. Again, in the southern hemisphere, these directions should be reversed.

- Tall and trellised crops: asparagus, corn, cucumbers, fava or bell beans, grains (such as wheat, quinoa, and oats), melons (see Chapter 8), peas, pole beans, and tomatoes
- Medium crops: most brassicas (such as broccoli, cauliflower, cabbages, kale, collards), celery, eggplant, garlic, leeks, okra, onions, peppers, potatoes, shallots, summer squash (such as zucchini and yellow crookneck), and Swiss chard
- Short and trailing crops: arugula, most herbs, kohlrabi, lettuces, radishes, root crops (such as carrots, parsnips, and beets), spinach, watermelon, and winter squash (such as pumpkins and acorn squash)

By placing shorter crops in front of (or to the south of) taller crops, all plants have access to full sun and won't compete or overtake one another. Let's take that same 4' x 8' (1.2 x 2.4m) raised bed and plan out the crops to be planted here.

TALL CROPS	Tomato	Tomato	Tomato	Cucumber	Cucumber
MEDIUM CROPS	Pepper	Pepper	Pepper	Eggplant	Swiss Chard
SHORT CROPS	Lettuce	Lettuce	Spinach	Radishes	Arugula

Note: Reverse this in the southern hemisphere.

Tallest to Shortest

Tall crops such as tomatoes and cucumbers, which can be trellised, are located in the back or at the north end of the raised bed. Medium crops, such as peppers, eggplant, and Swiss chard, are placed in front of the tallest crops, closer to the south. Finally, the shortest crops, like lettuces, spinach, carrots, radishes, and arugula, are placed in the southernmost part at the front of the raised bed. This allows all the vegetables to access full sun.

Strategically placed trellised cucumbers can be a source of shade for plants that need it.

Now, for the cool part—literally. This plant-placement method can also be used to strategize in hot weather to protect plants that can't handle extreme temperatures in the summer months. For example, lettuces bolt to seed quickly in hot weather, making them bitter and inedible. You can strategically grow cucumbers on a trellis in the middle of the raised bed, in the medium row, and then plant lettuces to the north or behind the cucumbers in the shadows of the plants. *Ta-daa!* A cucumber sun umbrella. The lettuces will stay cooler during hotter weather and resist the urge to peter out so quickly.

Planting short or trailing crops to the south also has a benefit. When it comes to trailing crops like pumpkins and watermelons, they can take over your entire garden without much effort. Usually, these trailing crops tend to grow toward the sun, so by planting them toward the south end of the raised bed, the vines will gravitate southward, into your pathways, instead of consuming precious space in your raised bed. This will leave room for other crops without sacrificing an entire bed. Vigorous plants will still attempt to sprawl all over the place, but you can easily move the vines out of the way because they only attach to the ground at the roots. **Note:** Pumpkins can produce roots along the vine, but if you are diligent in redirecting vines before they anchor new roots, it won't be a problem.

Special Considerations for Wildlife and Extreme Temperatures

If you live in foothills, mountainous areas, or recently developed areas where deer, raccoons, or ground-dwelling animals reside, you may need to take additional steps when setting up your garden. It's possible you'll need to construct fencing, underground barriers, or even a walk-in structure in order to protect your garden. If you're going to put in all the effort to grow some of your own food, you might as well reap the benefit of being able to harvest it all. And let's not forget household pets. A low barrier may not be enough to keep Scruffy from trampling your raised beds and eating your tomatoes (yep, they do that). Most of these protections will be discussed in Chapter 9, but keep this in mind as you plan out your gardening area.

If your region experiences frost or high temperatures for extended periods of time, you may want to include overhead protection for your crops. Desert communities often use shade structures to protect their plants from scorching during hot summers. Simple metal frames or PVC hoops can be covered with shade cloth to block out 30 to 70 percent of sunlight. When temperatures drop, you can replace the shade cloth with insulated garden fabric. We'll talk more about this in Chapter 2.

Deer and other woodland creatures can wreak havoc on a garden. Be prepared to protect what you grow.

CHAPTER 2

Garden Beds

Once you have your garden location, orientation, and general area planned, it's time to get to work on building the garden itself. This chapter will explain the reasoning behind using raised beds as well as the different options for materials. We'll also cover the specifics of how to build your garden beds and offer tricks for building beds that will last.

Why Raised Beds?

Raised beds are a great way to organize your garden; they offer a clear delineation between growing areas and pathways, but most of the benefits reach beyond aesthetics. In climates where the ground freezes in winter, raised beds are essential. By elevating the planting area above ground, the bed soil will thaw and drain more quickly in spring, allowing for an earlier start to your gardening endeavors.

If you have heavy clay soil (read more about that in Chapter 3), raised beds can alleviate the days of backbreaking labor required to set up a garden as well as condition the soil each year. Raised beds don't eliminate work altogether,

Raised beds at Gardenerd HQ allowed us to "rise above" the sandy, depleted native soil.

but they make it much easier to add compost and improve soil structure and tilth as time goes on. In some cases, once you've built your raised beds, you may never need a shovel again. A hand trowel will often suffice to work the soil and plant crops.

If you choose to set up your garden with raised beds, you will also notice that they save time and valuable resources. Raised beds concentrate the areas that need water, so rather than watering your entire garden area,

Vegetable garden beds don't have to be boring.

you're only watering what's in the raised beds. Because water is a precious resource, and droughts are predicted to become more frequent and long lasting in places that already experience them, it makes sense to put water only where it is needed. As a result, your pathways remain dry. Dry pathways mean fewer weeds, which equals less work for you. Mulch those pathways with wood chips or other biodegradable materials (newspaper, straw, and burlap sacks work well), and you will even further reduce the need to weed.

Raised beds are the method of choice for most biointensive gardening methods (more about those in Chapter 5) because they concentrate resources and allow a gardener to maintain the beds without walking on and compressing the soil. Raised beds are also handy for folks with lower-back issues or certain disabilities. The elevated surface area makes it easier to garden without bending over as far, and often you can even build beds tall enough to prevent bending altogether. Elevated raised beds (up on legs) can be built for wheelchair accessibility. If you have trees or hedges near your garden area, you can line your raised beds on the bottom to prevent thirsty tree roots from taking over your garden. See? The benefits really do go on and on.

Materials for Raised Beds

When it comes to deciding what materials to use for building a raised bed, you have a lot of options, depending on your budget and needs. If you strive to recycle and reuse found materials, then "urbanite" or broken concrete might be the way to go. If you're in a tight space, thinner materials that allow for the most gardening area with the least bulk—wood or composite lumber—are better choices. Let's take a look at the possibilities.

Wood

Wooden raised beds can be assembled quickly and last for years, depending on the type of wood you use. Douglas fir, which is relatively inexpensive, lasts about three to five years before it begins to decompose (though it can, in some circumstances, last for more than ten years in dry conditions). If you are building a simple frame for an experimental garden, or you plan to move in a few years, Douglas fir is good enough to use.

Redwood is a more durable option for wood-framed raised beds. It is an acidic wood, which makes it naturally antimicrobial. Redwood raised beds tend to last about 10 to 15 years longer than Douglas fir beds.

Cedar, which lasts 20 years or more, is a great option for long-term raised beds. It can be more expensive but is worth the investment if you plan to be in the same place for a while. Cedar resists decay and is often available as rough-cut lumber, which means it hasn't been milled down to the standard (think thinner) dimensions. The thicker wood is more rustic, but those extra millimeters make it even more durable.

Composite Lumber

Composite lumber is another option for planter beds. This type of material is a blend of recycled plastic packaging waste and wood pulp. It is extruded into the shape of wood and is usually used to build decks and patios. Many companies offer prefabricated raised beds made from nonleaching and soil-safe composite lumber, but be aware that not all composite lumber products are safe for direct soil contact. Trex® decking, made by Trex Company (*trex.com*), is one of the few composite lumbers that specifically states that it is safe for direct soil contact. Some composite lumbers begin to disintegrate when they come into

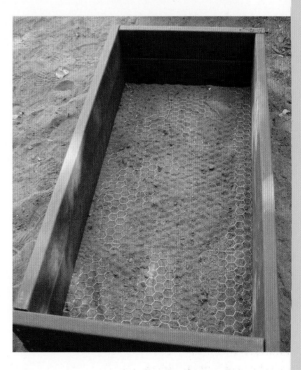

A raised bed made from two levels of 2" x 6" (5 x 15cm) Trex decking. With no known gophers in the neighborhood, we used chicken wire simply as a precaution. In the end, it was not necessary.

contact with soil. Veranda®, a thinner composite product found on the shelves of larger hardware stores, clearly states that it is not safe for direct soil contact.

Composite lumber has its advantages. It is long lasting (Trex is guaranteed for 25 years but is likely to last even longer), it won't splinter, and you never need to paint or stain it. The material costs about a third more than wood, but, given its durability, it's worth the expense to know that you won't have to build another raised bed for a very long time, if ever again. Composites are dense and heavy, so you may blow through a saw blade or two while cutting it, but in all other respects it cuts and behaves like wood.

Urbanite or Concrete Blocks

These are popular options for those who are looking to use recycled products. If you spy your neighbors breaking up their concrete driveway or sidewalk, ask if you can have the broken pieces. These concrete bits are great for building retaining walls that are thick and sturdy. They can also be used as paving material for pathways. If you decide to use urbanite to build a raised bed, however, be aware that it is usually 4"–6" (10–15cm) thick and can be cumbersome to climb over when reaching into a planting area. As mentioned before, wood offers the thinnest option for a raised bed, usually just 2" (5cm) thick. Blocks take up a lot more room, so if growing space is at a premium in your yard, opt for something thinner. That said, if you are looking to make raised beds that appear earthbound, solid, and hefty, urbanite or concrete blocks can create this look.

Cinder Block

Cinder block, like urbanite, is a substantial building material for raised beds. Unlike concrete, though, cinder block is made with fly ash, a waste product of the coal industry. While there is no official study proving this, it is speculated that heavy

Wooden posts and stones create a vegetable garden with Japanese overtones.

metals present in fly ash—namely arsenic, cobalt, lead, and mercury—will off-gas and leach into groundwater and soil. Gardening forums have countless discussions on this subject, with healthy arguments both for and against the use of cinder block, but it deserves further investigation if you plan to use this material.

Stones and Other Natural Materials

If you plan to grow mostly in-ground but still want to include some decorative elements of design along with a few extra inches (7–8cm) of garden soil, stones or other natural materials offer a lot of flexibility. No mortar is necessary unless you are building borders that are several layers high.

Cob and Adobe

These earthen materials are used to build houses, retaining walls, and other structures. Both use a mixture of sand, clay, and straw to form whatever shape is desired. To make these structures durable as raised beds, and able to withstand constant moisture and soil contact, lime is added to a finishing plaster as a sealant. Alternatively, adobe bricks are often found in gardens designed using permaculture principles and are an acceptable material for raised beds. Earthbags are another earth-based building material, often made from otherwise discarded, misprinted polypropylene bags. They simplify the building process: rather than making adobe bricks, you fill the earthbags with native soil (with as little as five percent clay) and stack them together. Earthbags can then be covered with a layer of adobe for a smooth finish. Some earthbag aficionados suggest coating the soil side of the new retaining wall with a layer of cement-based stucco plaster to help prevent degradation from excessive moisture.

Guidelines for Shape and Size

When building your garden beds, there are several other things to take into consideration. Will you have small children in the garden with you? Do you want to bring a wheelbarrow right up to a raised bed? Do you have or anticipate having back problems? Are you a card-carrying neat freak? The answers to these questions will help you determine the size and shape of your beds and how much space to leave between them.

Just How Neat Are You?

Let's start with the last question first. It might not seem like a factor in gardening, but an orderly space can make the difference between spending time in the garden or not. If you prefer to have everything in its place, but you now have an unorganized and random garden, you probably won't want to be there very often. A soldierly array of crisp raised beds might just be the ticket. Conversely, if you'd rather your vines ramble, and you love the look of a lush, overgrown jungle, take this into consideration before installing formal square beds. Chances are high that a snaking border or keyhole garden (see Part 2) is going to suit you better.

Evenly spaced and orderly is the way to go for some gardeners.

What Do You Want from Your Garden?

Your garden should match your needs. Do you want high production, or do you just want to putter around? If you intend for this garden to produce a bounty of food for your family, you will benefit from structuring the garden with beds in full sun along with easy-to-access pathways with room for a wheelbarrow or large tubs. Build your planter beds wide enough to accommodate large plantings but narrow enough so you can access the produce without stepping into the beds. If, on the other hand, this garden is going to be a place to disappear and putter, then feel free to create cluster gardens, perhaps each with a different theme, and choose locations around your yard to tuck them into. Making choices that satisfy your needs will help you enjoy and use your garden(s) more thoroughly. Let's look at some pointers for high-production gardens.

High-Production Gardens

Width: An adult can reach the center of a raised bed from either side most easily if the bed is no wider than 4' (1.2m). It can be as long as you want—4' (1.2m), 6' (1.8m), 12' (3.7m), or more—as long as you can access the midline of the bed on the two long sides. Some biointensive methods call for beds that are 5' (1.5m) wide. To prevent soil compression that can occur while working these beds, farmers and gardeners usually keep planks of wood on hand to distribute their weight evenly. By laying a plank down across the area, a person can step or kneel on the plank instead of directly on the soil.

Children can't reach as far as adults and will have to climb into your garden, disturbing the soil and possibly trampling seedlings if they can't reach the center. Limit kid-sized beds to 4' (1.2m) wide or less. A 3' (0.9m) wide bed will be sufficient for adults, while giving children room to grow. A 2' (0.6m) wide bed, while it may seem small, can be the perfect size for little hands in a school garden. While we're on the subject of kids, this is a good time to mention that toddlers are usually pullers or diggers. They love to grab tiny seedlings and get a closer look. They like to dig tunnels for their rubber duckies. If this makes the hair on the back of your neck stand up, you might want to create a special garden just for the kids.

Depth: Unless you have rich, loamy, fecund soil to begin with, you will want to build a raised bed that is at least 12" (30.5cm) deep. Adequate root space is critically important to a plant's health. Some gardening experts say that 6" (15cm) deep is plenty, but the truth is that the deeper the soil is conditioned, the more easily plants will grow. Give your garden a good head start by building a foundation that is deep enough. For those using wood for this task, 2" x 12" (5 x 30.5cm) lumber is best.

Pathways: An average gardener needs only 2' (0.6m) of space between beds to access the garden with ease. It is wide enough to kneel or sit down without backing into the bed behind you. If you plan to use a wheelbarrow or small garden cart, or need wheelchair access, make the pathways between beds at least 3' (0.9m) wide. Better

Plan your garden accordingly if you will have little helpers.

yet, measure your cart or wheelchair and base your pathway dimensions on that. Some experts reduce the amount of space between beds in order to fit more crops. If you are comfortable with navigating the foliage that will inevitably spill out of your incredibly productive beds onto the pathways, feel free to reduce the pathways to 19" (48cm) or less. Just be aware that melons and squash will make for an interesting obstacle course.

Low-Key Gardens

If you plan to have a more low-key, meandering garden instead, keep these principles in mind.

Stepping stones are your friends: No matter how you set up your garden, you will be able to manage it more easily if you place stepping stones in strategic places to help navigate around your growing areas. A well-placed piece of flagstone or tile can help direct wandering guests and help prevent soil compaction in conditioned beds. If you plan to have growing areas that are wider than 4' (1.2m), situate more stepping stones in the middle of the growing area to allow for ease of access.

Mimic nature: Nature presents itself in winding streams and spiraling vines. You can incorporate these elements of nature into the shape of your garden beds. A curving pathway through irregularly shaped beds can be more inviting to curious guests than a beeline entryway. You can also incorporate curves into the garden to capture water (more on that in Chapter 7). If you plan to create undulating, free-form shapes, it is much easier to use adobe or earthbags, rather than wood, to build your raised beds. Bricks and stones offer similar flexibility. Just make sure your materials are not so thick and bulky that you lose access to the planting areas. Check out the Keyhole Garden design idea in Part 2.

Where Will You Sit?

There are many ways to create sitting spaces in the garden, and raised beds offer a couple of different ways to rest. You can create a sitting rail around the perimeter of the bed by adding a "cap" of a 2x4 horizontally atop the frame of the bed. Secure the cap with 3" (7.5cm) wood screws and add vertical supports—usually also made from 2x4s—that run top to bottom on the outside of the raised bed, underneath the cap. Another option is to place your raised beds closer together with smaller pathways, so you can sit on the edge of one bed while working in the other. This strategy also helps those gardeners with lower-back issues. In Part 2, find detailed instructions on how to build raised beds, raised-bed building tips, and how to calculate the amount of soil you'll need.

A curving pathway can be both interesting and useful.

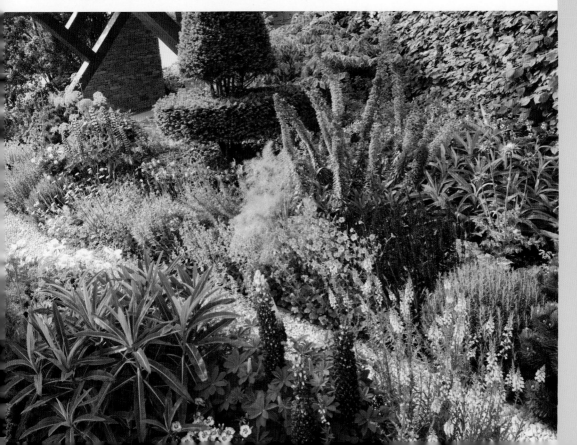

GARDENING TIP:
OLD-SCHOOL STRING LINES

When setting up mounded raised beds, place stakes at each corner of your target bed area and run string along the sides to map out clear lines for your beds. Whether you are building stacked mounds with layers of organic material or just hilling up soil and compost, these lines will ensure that your beds are straight.

Berm Beds

Often called *unconstructed beds* or *mounds*, berm beds are the right choice for those who want to build a garden without actually building anything—not even stacks of organic matter. These beds also allow for more creativity. They can be formed into any shape, length, and size to accommodate your grand garden vision. Do you want a snaking berm with sunflowers along the pathway? A circle mound for your potato patch? Start digging.

There are several ways to build an unconstructed bed. A common practice is to mark out the bed areas (see the Old-School String Lines tip above), but instead of digging inside the bed area, dig soil out of the pathways and dump it onto the bed areas. This leaves the pathways lower than soil level and the beds higher than where they started. This technique was used by indigenous cultures to irrigate their crops and is often used in commercial agriculture today. The lower pathways fill with water, and the water is absorbed at the base of the mounds. Plant roots reach deeper for water, making them more resilient and drought tolerant. In permaculture, a variation of the pathway-turned-trench is called a *swale* and is often used to divert water away from flood-prone areas toward plant-root zones (we'll talk more about this in Chapter 7). Turn to page 34 for other ways to build mounded beds, including "no-dig" beds.

Mounded raised beds are usually 4"–8" (10–20cm) tall, though some adventurous gardeners have been known to build them waist-high. Pathway soil is mixed with compost to create loamy, well-drained soil that will hold together in mounds. The sides are sloped, and the surface of the mound either is flat across the top or has a gentle convex curve.

The theory behind this kind of mounded bed is that it creates more surface area. Sloped sides plus a flat top equals more soil exposed to the sun, which means that the soil thaws and warms more quickly in spring. Some gardeners take advantage of the extra surface area by planting crops on the slopes of each bed. You gain up to another foot (30.5cm) of growing space if your beds are 6" (15cm) tall. Be aware that slopes can erode during watering, so keep the slopes, if not the whole bed, well mulched to retain water and prevent soil loss.

Mounded (berm) raised bed

In-Ground Planting

While unconstructed, or berm, beds are essentially the same as in-ground planting, the difference is height. An in-ground garden bed is made by loosening the existing soil of the desired planting area and working (digging) compost into the top 4"–6" (10–15cm). If you have existing soil that tends toward sand or loam, this is a fine choice. Those with clay soil will find it difficult to cultivate a garden this way without adding copious amounts of compost. In fact, clay soil is the reason raised beds were invented in the first place! Because clay soil doesn't drain well and takes longer to thaw after winter, use this method only if you have sandy, well-draining soil.

Be sure to test your soil before planting in the area. Most university agriculture departments offer basic soil tests, and some will test your soil for heavy metals. Do you know the history of the land you plan to cultivate? With all of these good intentions for healthier living, it would be a shame to inadvertently poison yourself by growing food in soil contaminated with heavy metals, so be safe and get that soil tested. We'll talk more about soil nutrients and heavy metals in Chapter 3.

Conditioning an in-ground planter takes about as much sweat and elbow grease as an unconstructed bed. Many first-time gardeners like to try this method before committing to a formalized garden layout. It doesn't require a lot of planning, just a lot of compost. Work the compost down into the top 4"–6" (10–15cm) of soil. The deeper you loosen and amend the soil, the better your crops will grow. You can add decorative elements, like stone or brick borders, and put stepping stones throughout the planter to avoid compacting the soil.

No matter what type of raised bed you decide to use, just know that good planning pays off. Your garden will reward you with a bountiful harvest if you put some time and energy into the overall design and structure. Build your beds once and enjoy them for years to come.

Mounds: Naturally Raised Beds

Simply put, a mounded raised bed is an aboveground pile of organic matter, usually with sloped sides. These beds are at least 6" (15cm) tall but can be up to 2' (61cm) tall, depending on the materials used. Some gardeners stick to soil and compost as ingredients, while others layer different "browns" and "greens" (see Part 2 for a list of these compostables), using a method often referred to as no-till, no-dig, lasagna gardening, sheet mulching, or the Stout System, in honor of Ruth Stout, author of *How to Have a Green Thumb Without an Aching Back*.

It's like building a compost pile straight in your garden, but then you plant in it. Start with newspaper, then add layers of browns and greens until the pile reaches 2' (61cm) tall, top it with compost, and water well. Ruth recommended using an 8" (20cm) layer of browns—basically any bulky material that could be used as mulch, such as hay, straw, sawdust, wood chips, or fall leaves. Her greens included garden waste, kitchen scraps, and grass clippings.

You can build a mound directly on your existing soil, but if you have a lawn or grassy (weedy) area, it's best to start with cardboard. Lots of it. One layer is not enough to kill Bermuda grass/crabgrass/devil's grass; think more like 5"–8" (13–20cm)

Mounded raised beds can be productive if you amend with plenty of compost first.

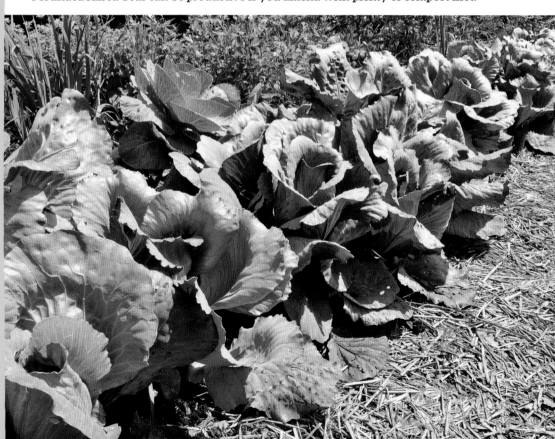

thick. That's a lot of cardboard. But let's say, for the sake of argument, that you have weed-free soil selected for your future garden area. You can skip the cardboard and start with a ¼"–½" (0.5–1.25cm) layer of newspaper. What does this do? Once wet and covered with other materials, decomposing newspaper creates the perfect environment, inviting microorganisms to break down the organic matter and till it into the soil for you. It provides carbon, which is one part of the compost equation. It will attract the right kind of fungi to your future garden, the kind that will help make nutrients available to your plants. Water the newspaper very, very well.

Contemporary versions of the Stout System start with newspaper or cardboard and then add a layer of alfalfa; this version starts with greens, meaning nitrogen instead of carbon. Nitrogen-rich materials attract beneficial bacteria to your garden, and they do the work to not only break down organic matter but also to provide food for other microbes that will arrive later. A bale of alfalfa naturally separates into 4" (10cm) layers, called flakes. While some people prefer to break up the flakes before layering, it's perfectly acceptable to use the compressed flakes on top of the newspaper. One 4" (10cm) layer is a good starting point. Again, saturate this layer with water.

For the brown/carbon layers, use twice as much material as your green layer. Variations on the lasagna-gardening theme range from adding bone meal, blood meal, or peat moss between each layer; to adding compost in the middle or bottom of the stack, instead of on top; to using ash or mulch as a finishing layer. It leaves a lot of room for experimentation, doesn't it?

All of these layering techniques require plenty of water as each layer is applied. Straw can take a very long time to become saturated, so be sure to use ample water while building your mounds or consider soaking materials ahead of time. Straw will become much heavier when wet, though, so keep the bale close to its final destination while soaking.

The philosophy behind this type of mounded garden bed is that, once established, the garden doesn't need water. Granted, its advocate, Ruth Stout, lived in Connecticut, where the average rainfall is 50" (127cm) per year. Gardeners in drought-ridden states will need to adjust for annual rainfall or the lack thereof. Another benefit of no-till gardening beds is reduced labor, and, as the beds decompose, they feed the soil beneath them. After a season or two, your garden soil will be much easier to dig if you decide you want to pick up a shovel.

CHAPTER 3

All About Soil

Soil is the foundation of every great garden. Without healthy soil, plants may grow, but they won't thrive. Plants take up all of their nutrients from the soil (plus the energy they get from the sun), and they need space to spread their roots, so it's important to create and maintain a healthy soil environment for your crops. What makes up a healthy soil environment? A lot of things. Let's take a look at the cast of characters.

Start with good soil and your plants will reward you by growing abundantly.

Nutrients

Soil contains a vast array of elements and minerals that play an important role in a plant's life. The "Big Three" are nitrogen (N), phosphorus (P), and potassium (K). Nitrogen is responsible for green, leafy growth. It's what makes your tomato plants grow big, green, and bushy. Phosphorus helps those tomato plants develop strong roots and, more importantly, make flowers that eventually turn into fruits (yes, a tomato is technically a fruit). Potassium, sometimes referred to as *potash*, helps support a plant's overall vigor as well as fruit development and disease resistance. Together, these three ingredients lend themselves to raising happy, productive vegetables.

The Big Three do not work alone, however. They have a supporting cast, an ensemble of minor characters that help make their work easier. Trace minerals, including calcium, sulfur, iron, magnesium, manganese, and boron, all have jobs to do. They help facilitate nutrient uptake to plants and perform specialized tasks such as forming proteins, catalyzing chlorophyll, and dividing cells. The Big Three may be the stars, but they can't perform at their best without the support of trace minerals.

pH

Your soil will likely be acidic or alkaline, and soil pH measures the degree of that acidity or alkalinity. On the acid side of the soil spectrum (about 4.5), plants such as camellias, blueberries, azaleas, and hydrangeas thrive. In fact, the more acidic your soil is, the bluer your hydrangeas. On the alkaline side (about 8.0), artichokes, mint, and asparagus do well. Most vegetables like to grow in an environment that borders a neutral pH, which is 7.0, with many varieties flourishing in a range between 5.5 and 7.5. Every crop comes with a recommendation of its preferred soil pH. This does not prohibit you from growing that crop in your soil if your pH is different. For example, tomatoes prefer a soil pH that is slightly acidic (6.2–6.8), but tomatoes will grow and can even thrive in soils with a pH that is more neutral or alkaline (6.8–7.2).

Changing the pH of your soil is not like changing the pH of your swimming pool. In a pool or spa, you just add a few chemicals, and—*poof!*—the pH is different. It doesn't work that way with soil. It can take years to alter the pH of your garden soil, so the best approach is to find plants that do well in your existing soil conditions. That said, we'll cover ways to amend your soil to increase acidity or alkalinity later in this chapter. Bottom line: Don't let your soil pH deter you from trying to grow a multitude of vegetables. Most crops will do well across the spectrum of soil pH levels.

pH RANGE FOR SOIL AND COMMON HOUSEHOLD ITEMS

Soil Texture

It's time for a very important question: When you stick a shovel in the ground, does it slide right in, or does it barely penetrate the soil? Your soil's texture is going to determine how hard you will have to work to get your garden ready for planting, or at least which type of planter bed you will use. With texture, there is also a spectrum, just as with the acid/alkaline spectrum, and your soil texture will fall somewhere along the spectrum between clay, silt, and sand. There are pros and cons for each.

Microscopically, clay soil is made up of small particles, with very little airflow between them. Clay soil tends to drain poorly and is difficult to dig. In spring, in places where the ground freezes over, clay soil takes much longer to thaw, drain, and become

THE SOIL FOOD WEB

In addition to soil nutrients and micronutrients, there is an entire world (or "underworld," in this case) of insects and microbial life forms in your soil that make the plant world go 'round. It's called the soil food web, and the fungi, bacteria, protozoa, earthworms, and nematodes all have a purpose—a job to do. They are the stagehands who make the show run flawlessly.

Dr. Elaine Ingham, a soil microbiologist and president of Soil Foodweb, Inc. (*soilfoodweb.com*), first wrote about and coined the term "soil food web" during her research on soil microbiology in the 1980s and '90s. Jeff Lowenfels and Wayne Lewis, while tipping their hats to Dr. Ingham, uncover this world in their book *Teaming with Microbes*. They deftly explain how plants not only take up nutrients but also "produce chemicals they excrete through their roots." The excretions or "exudates" are then consumed by fungi and bacteria, which in turn are consumed by protozoa and

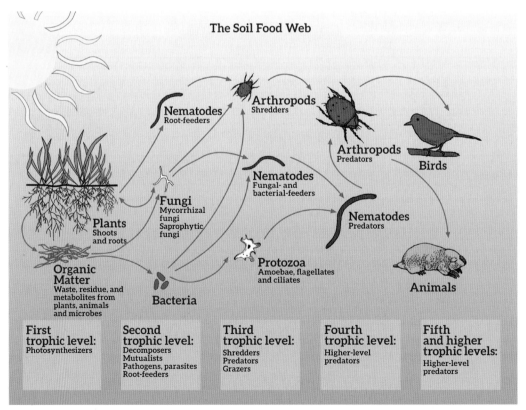

The Soil Food Web

Trophic means nutrition, with trophic levels referring to the steps in a food chain.

Root vegetables like these beets will grow well if you steward your soil food web.

nematodes, which then excrete waste that is taken back up by the plant as food. How convenient!

Don't forget the host of arthropods and insects, which burrow and aerate the soil, living and completing their life cycles (naturally or otherwise, i.e., being eaten by birds or other predators). When they die, their bodies go back into the food chain, breaking down into usable organic matter, which is once again consumed by microbes and, eventually, plants. This overlapping series of complicated food chains is the soil food web. It's fascinating stuff, but why does this matter to you as a gardener?

It matters because when your soil is healthy enough to support this intricate underworld of microbial activity, your garden will be more likely to thrive. Not only that—everything you do in the garden can help or hamper the soil food web. Every box of fertilizer, every shovelful of compost, every bottle of bug spray that is used on your plants affects this underworld. Don't worry, though, because we'll give you all the information you need to steward the microbial life in your garden's soil food web later in this chapter.

Home soil-testing kits test levels of nitrogen, phosphorus, and potassium as well as pH.

ready to work than sandy soil. Many gardeners avoid the whole process by building raised beds (turn back to Chapter 2 if you decide you want to do that). The benefit of clay soil is that it holds water and nutrients very well. Gardeners don't need to add fertilizer as often, nor do they need to water as much with clay soil, so it isn't all bad.

Sandy soil, on the other hand, is very loosely put together. Unlike clay soil, which forms into hard clods that are difficult to break up, sandy soil runs through your fingers and doesn't hold together if you try to form a clump. Under a microscope, you can see that it is made up of large particles. It's fantastically easy to dig, and it drains very well. The problem is that it drains too well. As a result, sandy soil loses moisture quickly—with all that fantastic drainage, away flows all of your carefully applied nutrients as well. Gardeners with sandy soil have to water more frequently and generally have to stay on top of adding amendments.

Silty soil behaves like a combination of clay and sand. The particles are larger than clay but nowhere near as large as sand. These particles characteristically feel silky, smooth like flour, or some even say greasy. Silty soil has a tendency to become compacted like clay, making drainage and digging difficult. Silt and sand are both made up of weathered rock particles, so they both respond to gravity in the same way—the particles will settle quickly in a water solution.

Get Tested

The first thing to do, before adding any fertilizers or soil amendments, is to get your soil tested. It takes a little time, and you have to wait for the results, but it's worth it. There are two kinds of tests available: basic and complete. A basic soil test reveals the nutrient levels of your Big Three. This type of test usually requires that you take a soil sample, mix it with water, and let it settle. Then you draw off some of the liquid and add it to a beaker with specific chemicals that are reactive to nitrogen, phosphorus, or potassium (this is the fun science part). Close the container, shake it, and then leave it undisturbed and wait for the color to change. You'll compare your results against a color chart to let you know how well supplied your soil is with that particular nutrient. You can buy basic soil tests for N, P, K, and pH at many nurseries or order them online through gardening catalogs.

The second type of soil test yields more elaborate results. A complete test involves sending a soil sample out to a laboratory. Soil technicians provide you not only with N, P, K, and pH ratings but also with ratings for trace elements, salinity, and heavy metals.

Why is this important? Well, let's say you live in a city, near a busy road. Your test might show high levels of zinc in the soil. Where did that zinc come from? Zinc disperses from braking systems on vehicles, from roads, from airplanes overhead, and from galvanized metal gardening tools (like watering cans or buckets). Excessive zinc prevents the uptake of nutrients in plants. That's right—it actually blocks the plant's ability to extract N, P, and K from the soil. A soil test might also show that the

Start a compost bin to turn garden and kitchen waste into a valuable soil amendment for your planter beds and containers.

pH of your excessively zinc-laden soil is acidic. This would tell you that, if you were to raise your soil's pH, you would bind up the zinc, making more nutrients available to your plants.

It's always a good idea to get a complete soil test to rule out the presence of lead (residues from turn-of-the-century oil drilling, leaded gasoline, and house paints), arsenic (used previously for years near railroads as a weed killer), mercury, cadmium, or aluminum. Most university departments of agriculture offer inexpensive soil tests (just search the internet for "university soil test" to find one near you), or you can send a sample to a soil lab, such as Wallace Laboratories (*wlabs.com*) in El Segundo, California. To find out the active microbiological composition of your soil (bacteria, fungi, nematodes, and more), look up "biological soil testing" or send a sample to a lab such as Earthfort (*earthfort.com*).

Make Amends

Once you know the nutrient levels of your soil, you can amend accordingly. Soil amendments—also called inputs—can increase available nutrients, but they also can alter soil texture or improve drainage. Let's revisit the soil textures: clay, silt, and sand. What can you do to improve these conditions?

Surprisingly, the organic solution to hard-packed clay soil, compacted silt, and loose, anemic sandy soil is one thing: compost. In clay and silty soil, compost serves to create space between particles and allow more airflow, which then helps the soil drain better. In sandy soil, compost works as a sponge to retain moisture and provides structure to hold nutrients. Compost brings these extreme conditions closer to the perfect texture for growing vegetables and fruits; this ideal is called loam. Loamy soil holds nutrients but drains well. It supports the easy proliferation of root systems and is nearly effortless to dig. Loam is the goal that every gardener hopes to attain with soil.

So how much compost should you apply to your soil? The general rule of thumb is to add compost in inches. Add a ½"–1" (1.25–2.5cm) layer at the beginning of each season before planting and, if needed, again during mid-season to boost production. You can either top-dress, meaning spread it out on the surface and leave it, or you can work it into the top few inches (7–8cm) of soil. Soil food web aficionados prefer to apply compost on the surface, without disturbing the delicate strands of fungal hyphae and microbial life hard at work in the soil. The microbes will utilize the compost as it filters through the soil during regular watering and as larger insects and earthworms till it into the soil for you. All of this activity makes nutrients available to plants with less work from you.

Gardeners with very sandy soil may choose to ignore the ½"–1" (1.25–2.5cm) rule of thumb and add compost with reckless abandon. It's OK. Add compost, then add more compost, and when you think you've added enough, add more. Your soil will be just about right at that point.

In addition to benefiting soil texture and structure, compost adds nitrogen and inoculates your soil with those stagehands we talked about earlier. Compost does much more than feed the soil; it brings it to life with fungi, bacteria, microscopic insects, and earthworms. It supercharges your soil with the microbiology needed to help plants thrive. You can buy bagged compost from nurseries, but why not make it yourself? It's a great way to recycle nutrients in your garden and cut down on waste that goes to the landfill. Food waste happens to be one of the top contributors to climate change, by the way. So if you aren't composting, now is a great time to start! Best of all, making your own compost means you know exactly what's in it, and you don't have to drive anywhere to get it. Turn to Part 2 for instructions on starting a compost bin, for active batch thermal composting techniques, and for a list of compost ingredients.

Fertilizers: Chemical, Organic, or None?

When it comes to fertilizers, there are three roads to take: use chemical fertilizers, use organic fertilizers, or don't use any fertilizers at all. It's an argument that's been going on since the mid-1950s between farmers who use conventional growing methods and those who farm organically. Permaculturists and some biointensive farmers would argue that nature provides its own fertilizer, so we don't need to add any inputs.

It's easy to be enticed by all of the options on the nursery shelves. Those boxes of fertilizer offer the promise of quick-fix solutions and gigantic, succulent vegetables. Some of them prove helpful, while others can cause long-term damage. Before you pour anything onto your soil, it's important to know what fertilizers do and why you might need them.

There is a lot of marketing hype about fertilizers. Don't be fooled. Your plants will thrive with natural fertilizer—these organic options are better for your soil and the environment.

This cover crop features hairy vetch, peas, oats, and more.

First, let's step back in history. Around the turn of the nineteenth century, farmers used one of two methods to fertilize their croplands:

- **Method 1:** They tilled in manure from farm animals or acquired copious amounts of horse manure from what was then known as the "transportation department" (think mounted police here). Farms were different then: they grew more than just one crop, and there were always plenty of animals around to contribute to soil fertility.
- **Method 2:** Farmers infused their land with nitrogen by growing a cover crop of legumes such as fava beans or peas. The fields were seeded with bean seeds, and after the crops had grown tall, farmers cut them down and dug the biomass into the soil. The biomass decomposed and improved the soil structure, but the magic was happening underground in the roots.

The air we breathe is 76% nitrogen. Legume crops have the ability to pull atmospheric nitrogen out of the air and lock it into the plants' roots. Here's how it works: Friendly bacteria called rhizobia (part of the soil food web) establish a home in the roots of leguminous plants. The bacteria are able to "fix" nitrogen in the roots, in the form of little pink nodules. When bean plants just begin to flower, the roots are full of these pink nodules. The crops are strategically cut down, and the roots are left in the soil to biodegrade, a process that eventually releases the fixed nitrogen into the soil. A farmer would then plant crops and enjoy the benefits of amply supplied nitrogen.

A third, unpredictable way to fix nitrogen into the soil as fertilizer was to hope for lightning. Lightning deposits hundreds of thousands of pounds of nitrogen into soil every year. It happens when the energy of lightning breaks the bonds of nitrogen molecules in the air. The particles mix with vapor and rain, fall to the earth, and are absorbed into plants and soil. This method is helpful but not enough to supply the full amount of fertilizer needed for most farmers.

Along came German chemists Fritz Haber and Carl Bosch, who figured out how to manufacture synthetic nitrogen. They did this in the early twentieth century by combining atmospheric nitrogen and hydrogen to create ammonia (widely used as ammonium nitrate in fertilizers today). The technique, the Haber-Bosch Process, was lauded as one of the most important inventions of the day, and it gave the farming community tools to solve world hunger. The German duo won Nobel Prizes for chemistry in 1918 and 1931.

The Issues with Synthetic Fertilizers

Despite the promise of increased yields, history has uncovered several issues with synthetic nitrogen.

Strike One: Not Sustainable. First of all, synthetic nitrogen is made from natural gas. Natural gas is a common source of hydrogen, and while that makes it easy for mass industrial production, it's a natural resource with a finite supply and an extraction method that contaminates groundwater and causes air pollution.

Strike Two: Effect on Water. The next thing to consider is how much nitrogen, synthetic or otherwise, is actually taken up by plants. Much like humans, who absorb nutrients in minute quantities over time, plants take up only a small amount of nitrogen, in much lower doses than synthetic brands of fertilizer provide. A box on the nursery shelf might list the Big Three (N, P, K) ratios as 20–20–20 or 30–30–30. Those are very high numbers when it comes to fertilizer.

Think about this: What happens when you take a multivitamin? Your body absorbs some of it, but what happens to the rest? It flushes away. The same is true for plants. Nitrates that aren't absorbed will bind to water molecules and will release down into the water table. Once there, it travels out to sea through waterways. Rivers and bays with excess nitrates develop algae blooms because, remember, nitrogen is responsible for green, leafy growth. Algae are hungry for oxygen and rob the water and fish of that life-giving resource. The result is a dead zone. Strike two against synthetic nitrogen.

Strike Three: Effect on Soil. Nitrates are very high in salts. High salinity diminishes a plant's ability to take up water, which causes stress and stunted growth and can eventually kill a plant. Arguments have been made, even by reputable soil scientists, that plants can't tell the difference between organic and synthetic nitrogen. While it may be true that the plants may not be able to tell the difference, your soil can. Study after

Synthetic fertilizer leads to more nitrogen runoff, causing algae blooms in waterways, so use only what is needed to fertilize your garden.

study has shown that high-salinity, high-nitrate fertilizers reduce populations of soil microbes. It diminishes your soil food web. OK—some types of soil biology may survive the onslaught, but the overall system will take a hit. If you worked hard to create your ecosystem both above and below ground, to create an environment where nature does much of the work for you, take a moment to consider what synthetic fertilizers do to the soil before you apply them.

The Benefits of Organic Fertilizers

Now, let's talk about organic fertilizers. These amendments range from plant-based materials such as alfalfa, to minerals such as rock phosphate, to animal by-products such as bone meal. Each has its own properties, and typically several nutrients are combined to create "balanced" fertilizers for different plant groups. On nursery shelves, you will find a box of fertilizer for vegetables, one for roses, another for acid-loving plants, and yet another for fruit trees. Each brand has a proprietary blend that it feels is best for its customers. The blend of nutrients appears on the box as the ratio of our Big Three, and those numbers will range between 3 and 7—much lower than synthetics. For example, a box of organic citrus fertilizer may list a ratio of 7–4–2, meaning that the total content of each nutrient is 7% nitrogen, 4% phosphorus, and 2% potassium.

Remember: More is not necessarily better. While synthetic fertilizers look better by the numbers, a good portion of the synthetic fertilizer will not be absorbed by the plant. Excessive fertilizers can burn plants and contaminate nearby waterways, causing harm to the nearby wildlife. The lower amounts of nutrients in organic fertilizers are actually a benefit: they balance helping your plants without hurting anything else.

Another benefit? Organic fertilizers don't negatively affect soil biology. In fact, the microbes and earthworms that are nutrient-cyclers consume the organic inputs and convert them into nutrients that give back to the plant. This keeps both your Soil Food Web and plants alive and healthy.

Available Nutrient Options in Fertilizer
Nitrogen: Green Leafy Growth

Animal-based sources of nitrogen include blood meal, feather meal, hoof and horn meal, and fish meal, which generally have a rate of 9%–15% in pure form. Both hoof and horn meal and fish meal also contain some percentage of phosphorus, fish meal being higher. Blood meal and feather meal may have little to no phosphorus, depending on its source.

Nonanimal-based sources of nitrogen are alfalfa meal, cottonseed meal, soybean meal, and kelp meal. These fertilizers offer a lower rate than their animal-based counterparts, between 1% and 7%. Another great source of nitrogen can be found in your coffee maker. Spent coffee grounds supply nitrogen at a rate of about 2%, with trace levels of phosphorus and potassium. Compost is a source as well, but it may surprise you that compost is relatively low in nitrogen. However, as we discussed earlier, plants take up nutrients in small amounts, so the available nitrogen is sufficient in many cases.

Spent coffee grounds provide 2% nitrogen, meaning you can "get" fertilizer from your trashcan . . . for free!

Plus, with the bonus of the vibrant, nutrient-building microbial life forms that compost provides, it makes a fantastic fertilizer.

Animal manures, which straddle the aforementioned categories—being from animals but not by-products of slaughter—are higher in nitrogen when dried, according to North Carolina State University research. Dried cow, chicken, and hog manures and fresh rabbit manure all provide nitrogen at a rate between 1% and 2.2%.

Phosphorus: Roots, Fruits, and Flowers

Bone meal is the predominant animal-based source of phosphorus, but, as mentioned, many of the animal-based nitrogen fertilizers also supply some phosphorus. Bone meal supplies phosphorus at a rate ranging from 11%–22%.

Rock phosphate and soft rock phosphate are nonanimal sources of phosphorus. They are both mined from sedimentary rock: rock phosphate as tricalcium phosphate, and soft rock phosphate as a by-product of the mining industry. They supply 2%–3% phosphorus. Both are widely available from nurseries and garden centers.

In the manure category, seabird or bat guano is excellent. These resources range from 10%–15% phosphorus and also have 1%–3%. However, bat guano has fallen from the list of recommended sources for two reasons: 1) the process of harvesting guano from caves has caused harm to bat populations, and 2) the dust can contain fungal spores that, if inhaled by humans, can cause a respiratory disease called histoplasmosis. Seabird guano is collected from islands off Peru uninhabited by humans, where it never rains and the guano piles up. It is labor-intensive because it must be harvested by hand, according to strict regulations. Workers scrape and gather guano when seabirds are not present. Many fertilizer companies offer both products at nurseries and online.

IS IT ORGANIC?

Even if that box of fertilizer says "organic," it doesn't mean that the source of that bone meal or manure was raised organically. It just means that the fertilizer was derived from organic matter.

Potassium: Overall Vigor and Fruit and Flower Development

Animal-based fertilizers supply virtually zero potassium, so we'll skip right to nonanimal-based options. Sulfate of potash, also known by the commercial name Sul-Po-Mag (meaning sulfate of potassium-magnesia) is the most common source of potassium. Potassium remains in the soil for years, so make sure that you test your soil first before applying, because it may not need potassium. Other options include greensand, which supplies between 3% and 7% potash. It is marine sediment mined from ocean-adjacent rock formations. If you have very sandy soil, avoid greensand because it will make soil texture even sandier. Kelp meal and liquid kelp emulsions generally supply low levels of potassium but offer the benefit of trace minerals as well. Wood ashes, depending on what is burned to create them, can provide small amounts of potassium and phosphorus. Don't use wood ashes if you have highly alkaline soil because it tends to raise pH.

Animal manures, both in dried and manure tea forms, supply potassium as well as the other aforementioned nutrients. Like liquid kelp emulsions, animal manures and manure teas also supply a broad spectrum of trace minerals.

pH Adjusters and Trace Minerals

Trace minerals play a role in nutrient uptake, and, depending on geographic location and farm practices, these minerals can become depleted. As mentioned, some organic fertilizers supply a small amount of trace minerals, so a fertilizer may be all you ever need to use. But you might be wondering what all of those other boxes on the nursery shelves are for. It's important to know what they are and what they do before applying them to your garden. Often, products that provide trace minerals also serve as soil pH adjusters. They will raise or lower your pH, and sometimes this is a good thing. Sometimes, not so much.

Limestone and dolomitic lime both raise soil pH, but calcitic or high-calcium lime, not surprisingly, supplies calcium as well. Dolomitic lime adds calcium and magnesium. For soils that have plenty of magnesium, it is recommended to use calcitic lime instead of dolomitic lime to raise soil pH.

Gypsum is often used to break up clay soils and contains calcium and sulfur in moderate amounts. The sulfur in gypsum also lowers pH. If you have soil pH that is already lower than 5.8, do not use gypsum.

The trouble with many soil and pH modifiers is that sometimes they solve one problem while creating another. Gypsum is the perfect example. It can lower the soil

DID YOU KNOW?

Let's pause for a mind-blowing scientific fact: Your soil's pH is controlled by plant exudates, and pH is altered by soil microbes and their relationship to the plants they support. Yep, it's true. Plant roots exude sugars and acids to encourage either bacterial or fungal growth. Bacterial populations convert these sugars and acids into compounds that drive soil pH up toward alkalinity. Fungal populations convert plant exudates into compounds that lower soil pH. Plants basically feed the microbes to create the environment they need for survival. For example, grasslands foster bacterial-dominant soil that is alkaline. Forests foster fungal-dominant soil that is acidic. So it's important to understand that if you steward your soil food web properly, plants will be able to adjust the soil pH on their own, without heavy-handed inputs.

The one exception just might be glacial rock dust. Even purist permaculture experts and devout biodynamic practitioners hail the stuff as a "wonder amendment." It is a by-product of the quarry industry and comes mostly from the process of cutting and polishing granite. It remineralizes depleted soils with a broad spectrum of trace minerals like calcium, magnesium, iron, and micronutrients. It does not significantly modify soil pH, but it is typically alkaline. What's more, beneficial soil microbes like it too, and worms find it handy to have around—they ingest it as grit in order to process food. Farmers and home gardeners have seen dramatic increases in production by amending the soil with glacial rock dust. Glacial rock dust is available from many garden centers, nurseries, and online farm supply stores.

The right balance of nutrients, micronutrients, and minerals—such as what's found in glacial rock dust—boosts your garden's growing potential.

Add nutrient-dense worm castings to your soil to help plants grow and to fight pests.

pH, making unwanted heavy metals like zinc more available to plants (remember, excessive zinc blocks nutrient uptake). Gypsum can also raise the salinity of soil, tipping the balance and disrupting soil microbial life. Limestone adds minerals but raises pH, which alkaline soils don't need. Investigate these soil modifiers thoroughly and get a soil test to be certain you need these trace minerals before adding them. Oh, and word to the wise: **don't use gypsum recycled from drywall**. Drywall contains ingredients like petrolium-based waxes, fiberglass, plasticisers, and mold-inhibitors.

Worm Castings

Also known as the other "black gold," worm castings prove that big things come in small packages. Worms ingest your kitchen scraps and garden waste then leave behind castings (a nice way of saying poop). Those castings are full of nutrients and can be used to fertilize your garden plants. Be aware that a little bit goes a long way. Jeff Lowenfels shared this statistical information about worm castings in *Teaming with Microbes*: "They have ten times the available potash; five times the nitrogen; three times the usable magnesium; and they are one and a half times higher in calcium . . . than soil that has not been through an earthworm." There's another component to worm castings that makes them a superior fertilizer. Let's dive into the science.

Worms don't have teeth. They have enzymatic mouthparts instead. The enzyme they use to break down food is called chitinase (pronounced KY-ti-năs). Chitinase also breaks down chitin, which happens to be an important component of insect exoskeletons. Chitinase is excreted in worm castings, and when you fertilize your plants with castings, the plants take up the chitinase enzyme. When pests nibble or suck on the now-chitinase-laced plants, they start to wonder why they're falling apart—they're eating an enzyme that dissolves their exoskeletons! So worm castings aren't just a great fertilizer, they solve pest problems like white fly and mealy bug too.

Having a worm bin not only helps produce your own castings for fertilizer and pest control, but it also gets rid of kitchen scraps. A worm can consume half its body weight in food scraps every day. So if you have 1 pound (450g) of worms in a bin, you can safely assume that your worms will be able to put away ½ pound (225g) of food scraps each day. That's about 3½ pounds (1.6kg) per week! Sure, you can buy the bagged stuff at a nursery, but the way to know for certain that you have viable, microbially active, enzymatic-rich castings is to make them yourself, just like compost. The benefit of eliminating food waste is a bonus. For instructions on how to make a worm bin, see Start a Worm Bin in Part 2.

Basic Fertilizer-Application Tips

To apply any of these fertilizers, follow the suggested amounts and directions on the packaging. Use the appropriate amount to prevent runoff and keep an eye on your plants to see how they respond. Whichever of these fertilizers and soil modifiers you decide to use in your garden, mix them well into the soil before planting. Plant roots prefer not to come in direct contact with fertilizers, so avoid throwing a handful into a planting hole and then plopping down your transplant unprotected. Mix amendments so they are well blended and then plant your veggies and seeds. If you've decided after planting to add these amendments, mix them first with compost, spread them around your plants, and scratch them into the top few inches (7–8cm) of soil.

✳✳✳

As you can see, soil is a big subject with plenty of nuance. Now that you have an understanding of what's going on in your underground ecosystem, it's time to move on to strategic planning in the garden.

CHAPTER 4

Planning Your Garden Season

I t's a ritual that happens every year: seed catalogs begin to appear in mailboxes, graph paper and pencils come out from hiding, and dreams of bountiful harvests propel gardeners forward into the growing season once again. There are so many seed varieties to try—how and where will they all fit in the garden? When should you plant? And what the heck is crop rotation? This chapter will help you figure out your growing season—or seasons—as well as what to plant in each. It will also give you some helpful tips to ensure the continued health of your garden and soil.

Find Your Frost Dates

Nature has a way of putting an end to summer gardens. It's called frost. Most climates have a first and a last frost. The range of time when planting is either safe or unsafe is marked by frost dates. When

Include diversity in your garden plan.

For the sake of your plants, know the frost dates of your region. Some plants can be protected and continue to produce before the weather gets too cold.

you don't have a frost (think warm-winter climates like coastal Los Angeles), frost dates have little or no meaning. For everyone else, it's life or death in the garden. Knowing your frost dates helps to ensure success each growing season. Here's a basic primer:

- **First frost**—This is the day that everyone dreads in fall. It means the end of the gardening season for most unprotected gardens. That frost comes through and wipes out most plants (some can survive with protective garden fabric covers, and some even thrive after a frost—e.g., kale and parsnips become sweeter). Most first-frost dates occur between September and November in the northern hemisphere (March through early June in the southern hemisphere).

- **Killing frost**—This consists of a drop in temperature to the point that freezes water. The cells of plants are full of water, and when water freezes, it expands. When water in cells expands, it ruptures the cells, essentially killing the plant. Not every frost is a killing frost. In fact, some climates make it through winter with only a light frost.

- **Last frost**—This is the day everyone awaits in spring. It's the reported average date after which a killing frost is not likely to occur. Most seed packets bear instructions telling you to "start seeds indoors six to eight weeks prior to last frost." That way, plants are ready to go into the ground once the threat of frost has passed. Last-frost dates usually fall between March and May in the northern hemisphere (August and September in the southern hemisphere).

To find your frost dates, you can ask your local university agriculture department or a neighbor who has been gardening for a few years. There are online resources where you can look up your frost dates by zip code; a popular one is found on the National Gardening Association's website (*garden.org/apps/frost-dates*). The website lists spring and fall frost dates with probability ratios that decrease as the season progresses. For example, Aliceville, Alabama, has a 90 percent chance of spring frost around March 27, but a 50 percent chance of frost around April 10, and only a 10 percent chance by April 24. It would be safe to assume that planting after April 24 is fine, and your plants might be OK if you planted them after April 10. It's a 50-50 chance. If you want to take the risk, use insulated garden fabric to protect crops, and your plants will most likely be fine.

Another website offers a simpler view of frost dates by simply typing in your zip code. *The Old Farmer's Almanac*, a longtime favorite resource of many home gardeners, uses the National Climatic Data Center's database but keeps it short and sweet: *almanac.com/gardening/frostdates*. Either website allows you to learn more about your frost dates.

What to Plant Each Season

This is the fun part. Once you know your frost dates, you will know whether you have one growing season or more. Climates that experience killing frosts generally plant crops from spring through fall and shut down the garden for winter. Those who have a greenhouse or other protected environment for crops can learn to surmount the challenges of winter gardening. Warm-winter climates that get light or no frost can grow year-round. So, take a look at your growing season and figure out how many frost-free days you'll have to work with. From there, decide what you want to grow.

Cool-Season Crops

In climates with frosts, these are vegetables that prefer to grow in early spring, before summer's heat kicks in. Seed packets for these veggies will often instruct you to "start

Cool-season crops include broccoli, Swiss chard, mustard greens, cilantro, green onions, lettuces, and cabbage.

six to eight weeks prior to last frost." How long your cool season lasts depends on those frost dates. In warm-winter climates, and places without frosts, these crops can be planted in spring, but they tend to do better if planted in late summer or early fall. They will thrive over winter until it's time to plant warm-weather crops in spring.

Warm-Season Crops

As spring temperatures rise, some plants prefer warmer soil and sun exposure to thrive or even to germinate. These are good transition crops as the season progresses.

Hot-Season Crops

These are the quintessential summer favorites that most gardeners look forward to growing each year. They typically require warm soil to germinate and higher temperatures to set fruit.

COOL-SEASON CROPS

- Arugula
- Beet
- Broccoli *
- Brussels sprout *
- Cabbage *
- Carrot
- Cauliflower *
- Celery *
- Chard
- Collard greens
- Cover crops
- Fava bean (direct-sow)

- Garlic (direct-sow cloves)
- Grains—quinoa, spring wheat, rye, amaranth
- Green onion
- Herbs—all but basil
- Kale
- Kohlrabi*
- Leek
- Lettuce
- Mesclun mix

- Mustard greens
- Onion
- Parsnip
- Sugar snap/snow pea
- Potato (from sprouted potatoes)
- Radish
- Rutabaga
- Shallot
- Spinach
- Turnip

(*start indoors or buy transplants)

Note: The cool season is also a great time to plant strawberries, fruit trees, artichokes, and asparagus crowns. Gardeners in warm-winter climates can plant those in fall. Also in warm-winter climates, late fall or early winter is the time to plant bare-root fruit trees, roses, and cane berries. These crops will work to develop roots over winter and will then be able to focus on top growth when spring temperatures arrive.

Warm- and hot-season crops include strawberries, cucumbers (lemon and early Russian shown here), cherry tomatoes, and zucchinis.

WARM/HOT-SEASON CROPS

- Basil
- Bush/pole bean*
- Corn
- Cucumber* (start indoors or plant starts later)
- Eggplant*
- Lettuce (direct sow or transplant with protection in hot weather)

- Lima bean*
- Muskmelon
- Okra*
- Pepper* (start indoors or plant starts later)
- Summer squash*— zucchini, yellow crookneck, etc.
- Sweet potato (from slips)

- Tomato* (start indoors from seed or plant starts later)
- Watermelon*
- Winter squash*— pumpkin, acorn, butternut, etc.

(*indicates hot-weather crops)

Note: Warm- and hot-season crops grow best from late spring through early fall. Plants should be well established before scorching temperatures set in, as some crops—like tomatoes—won't set fruit if temperatures are over 90°F (32°C). The flowers will drop off instead. Plan accordingly to make sure you have room for these summer sizzlers.

Keep the Family Together

As we discussed in Chapter 1, plant placement is all about strategy. You can plant tall crops to the north and shorter crops to the south to ensure that everybody is getting the sunlight they need. You can strategize to plant tall crops in front of short crops to provide some shade for cool-weather vegetables as they mature in warmer weather. These are great tools to have in your pocket, but there are a couple of other things to keep in mind as you plan out your garden.

Plants have families—or, rather, they belong to families. When you plot out the location for each crop, it's a good idea to keep these families together. Why? Because some plant families take up certain nutrients from the soil and others can leave behind diseases that can later be picked up by another member of the family that is planted in the same place year after year. See where we're going with this? Gardeners have good memories, but there's no need to tax the system (aka your brain) by planting a broccoli here, a broccoli there, a broccoli everywhere. Since those broccoli plants are in danger if they are planted where you previously planted broccoli within three years, it's much easier to move a plant family to a new location if you keep plants in that family grouped together in the first place. Plant families together to make crop rotation easier in the future.

Let's look at some of the families in the vegetable kingdom. I've used common names here to introduce them.

- **Cole crops (Brassicaceae)**—Often called brassicas, this family includes broccoli, cauliflower, cabbage, brussels sprouts, kohlrabi, and kale. It also includes turnip, radish, and mustard greens. If you need a hint to keep it straight, they all form bright little yellow flowers when they go to seed.

Cauliflower, cabbage, and broccoli are among the more popular brassicas.

- **Nightshades (Solanaceae)**—Vegetables in this family include tomato, pepper, eggplant, tomatillo, and potato. Tobacco is also part of this family—think of it as the black sheep.
- **Alliums (Amaryllidaceae)**—The ever-popular onion family includes leek, onion, garlic, shallot, and chive.
- **Squash (Cucurbitaceae)**—Cucurbits, as plants in this family are often called, include cucumber, melon, winter and summer squash, watermelon, and gourds. By the way, summer squash grows in the summer, as does winter squash. The name refers not to when it is grown, but when it needs to be consumed and how long it stores. Summer squashes such as zucchini and yellow crookneck have thin skins that can easily be pierced with a thumbnail, so they have to be eaten shortly after picking. Winter squashes like pumpkin and butternut have thick skins that cannot be pierced with a thumbnail, so they can be stored over winter, thus the name winter squash.
- **Carrot (Apiaceae or Umbelliferae)**—Every plant in this family is an umbel, which means that when it goes to seed, it forms an umbrella-shaped flower. Dill, parsley, cilantro, fennel, celery, carrot, and parsnip all belong to this family.
- **Beet (Amaranthaceae or Chenopodiaceae)**—Do you like quinoa? Never heard of it? It's part of the beet family along with beets, chard, spinach, orach mountain spinach, and mangel. The two families mentioned in parentheses were merged, so now

amaranth is also included. Plants in this family tend to extract lead from soils, so if you've tested positive for high amounts of lead in your soil, lay low on the beet family.

- **Bean/pea (Fabaceae/Leguminosae)**—Chili wouldn't be the same without the members of this family, which include peas, lentils, beans, fava beans, a host of other dry beans, and peanuts. These crops, when cut down in the flowering stage, leave behind nitrogen for the next round of plants to feed upon. This family is an important part of sustainable gardening practices.

Delicata, acorn, and other winter squashes make a great centerpiece in the fall because they have thick skins that will last.

Crop Rotation for Healthy Soil

There are a number of reasons to rotate crops in a healthy garden. As mentioned, different crops pull different nutrients (or different levels of nutrients) out of the soil, and they can leave behind diseases, pathogens, or even pests. By planting a broad selection of vegetables, fruits, and herbs in your garden, and rotating those crops each season to a different spot, the likelihood of diseases, pests, and soil depletion is much lower.

Unlike farmers who grow acres and acres of one crop, also known as monocultures, you have the opportunity to garden sustainably with biodiversity. Biodiversity simply means a variety of life-forms in your garden—much like Chapter 1's ecosystem. A greater diversity of plants helps decrease the chances of future disease and pest infestations. Biodiversity also eliminates monoculture's main problem: taxing the soil beyond its capabilities. It's the opposite of putting all your eggs in one basket. That's smart gardening.

Another reason to rotate crops is to close the loop on inputs. Strategic crop rotation can help put nutrients back into the soil after one crop pulls them out. Some crops are heavy feeders, meaning that they consume a lot of nutrients in order to grow and produce fruit. Other crops give back to the soil, replenishing nitrogen and breaking down into beneficial organic matter that helps rebuild soil structure or provides biomass for the compost pile. Plants that fix nitrogen are heavy givers. By rotating heavy feeders with heavy givers, you will greatly reduce the amount of fertilizer and other inputs needed to garden sustainably.

John Jeavons of Ecology Action has spearheaded nearly 50 years of research on sustainable agriculture. In his book, *How to Grow More Vegetables*, he discusses the importance of crop rotation for nutrient recycling. "For many years, Ecology Action often followed a heavy-giver, heavy-feeder, light-feeder, low-nitrogen-lover type of crop rotation approach," Jeavons writes. Now, they use a simpler approach of planting cover crops (heavy givers) followed by heavy feeders, followed by a legume crop that is grown to maturity. When legumes are grown to the point that they form beans or peas, all of the nitrogen that has been stored in the plant during early growth is transferred to the beans. So the plant doesn't technically pull nitrogen from the soil; instead, it uses its own resource. Jeavons calls this period of the rotation the "soil nitrogen resting" phase. While there appears to be a difference of opinion about which plants are heavy or light feeders, here are some examples of each:

- **Heavy feeders**—tomato, corn, eggplant, brussels sprouts, and squash
- **Light feeders**—Swiss chard, sweet potato, leek, carrot, and parsnip
- **Heavy givers (if cut down during flower stage)**—fava beans, alfalfa, peas, clover
- **Legume crops for nitrogen resting**—most bean and pea varieties

However you decide to rotate your crops, choose a diversity of plants to include in your garden. The rewards will be paid out over years of successful harvests.

Quinoa is the gateway grain, meaning it's easiest to grow if you are interested in growing grains.

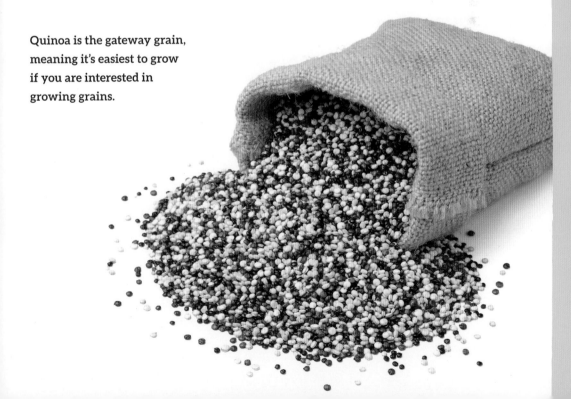

Companion Planting

When plotting out your garden, the next thing to consider is who to put next to whom. Companion planting is an age-old practice of grouping together plants that get along well and separating plants that don't. Do plants really care? Apparently, they do. There are plenty of studies that debunk companion planting but just as many that support it. With all the controversy, why not take it with a grain of salt but use the principles of companion planting to your advantage? You may see some benefits.

Louise Riotte first wrote about companion planting in *Carrots Love Tomatoes: Secrets of Companion Planting for Successful Gardening* in 1975. Her book sits on the shelves of thousands of gardeners who crack it open each year during spring planning. Along the same lines, *Companion Planting Made Easy* was published in 1995 as part of a series of publications on successful organic gardening. Both texts corroborate the partnerships we'll discuss here, but this just skims the surface of the pond. If you really want to dive into companion-planting lore, check out those books. There is such a large web of favorable companion connections that it's hard to keep it straight, especially when you add in what plants don't like.

Here are some examples of good companions, as well as kids who don't play well together.

Favorable Partnerships:

- Cole crops get along with onions, potatoes, and celeries.
- Beet-family crops like onions, lettuces, and cabbages.
- Bean/pea crops enjoy the company of cucumbers, and cucumbers like beans and peas right back.
- Pole beans help corns (think "three sisters" gardens).

Unsavory Connections:

- Cole crops don't care for strawberries or tomatoes.
- Beet-family crops don't get along with pole beans.
- Bean/pea crops dislike members of the onion family.
- Cucumbers and other squash-family members dislike potatoes.
- Fennel hates everyone. Plant that in a corner away from your other crops.

So why do some plants get along while others don't? Let's look at some of the reasoning behind it using some of these examples.

Pole beans and corn have a mutually beneficial relationship because corn is a heavy feeder and pole beans fix nitrogen into the soil. Meanwhile, corn reportedly decreases the presence of leafhoppers that attack bean plants. Beans and peas dislike onions (is it the bad breath?), but onions help most other crops grow well because their odor repels insects. Some sources say to keep beans away from peppers because they are both susceptible to anthracnose. Likewise, tomatoes and corn should be planted away from each other because the tomato fruitworm and the corn earworm are one and the same pest. Tomatoes and potatoes, both members of the Solanaceae family, are best kept apart because they are susceptible to blight, which can spread easily from one to

Cabbage and spring onions are "friends" in the garden.

the other. But, wait—aren't we supposed to keep plant families together? You can see how this companion-planting business can get confusing.

When planning your garden, keep a trusted set of books, including one on companion planting, close by (see the Bibliography and Resources section at the end of the book). Rather than memorize all of these plant combinations and aversions, it's much easier to flip through a book to confirm a hunch. Over time, you'll start to remember which plants are friends or foes, and you will be able to experiment with plant combinations to see what works in your garden.

What's in Your Pencil Case?

When you get right down to it, gardening takes planning. Now that you have the guidelines for laying out a successful garden, it's time to put it all down on paper. Yes, paper. It may sound old school, but nothing anchors an idea better than writing it down. The act of putting pen—or, in this case, pencil—to paper is a creative process like any art form. Here's what you'll need:

Space

It may be your kitchen table or desk, but you might need more room than that to spread out all of your seed catalogs and packets. Hint: floors and beds make great workspaces. Lay everything out in visual range so you can reference them as needed.

Catalogs and Seed Packets

You may have a collection of seeds that need places in the garden this season. The best way to know what you need to plant is to have those seeds close by. While you're at it, check to make sure you have enough of each variety. The catalogs are there to inspire and to replenish supplies. Gardenerds typically have pages dog-eared, hopeful that they will have spots for a new

Seeds open the door to growing rare and unusual plants.

variety or two. Group your seeds by plant family. It will come in handy when it's time to plot out crop locations.

Graph Paper or Template

Graph paper makes it easy to define raised beds, rows, or square feet. Instead, you may prefer to print up a blank template of your garden beds on your computer each season. If you don't plan on changing the shape of your garden each year, this might be the way to go.

Pencil and Eraser

Planning a garden is like completing a crossword puzzle. With all the different things to consider—companion planting, crop rotation, height, and sprawl—you're bound to make a couple guesses or mistakes. Go for the mechanical pencil; it has a fine point for writing in small spaces. Skip the puny eraser at the end of your pencil. You'll want the big guns for this: a white vinyl drafting eraser.

Ruler

A straight edge of some kind is always helpful when drawing garden beds or measuring out square feet. If you don't have a ruler, use a notepad with cardboard backing or any other straightedge in the house.

Gardening Books

Keep this book close by (of course) as well as books on companion planting and biointensive gardening methods (we'll cover those in the next chapter). Once you're solid on the crops that work in your climate, you may not need to refer to your books as often.

Put It All Together

Draw your garden space, raised beds, planters, and so on, and then indicate where north is relative to the beds. Now you're ready to plug in plant varieties in each one. Start with tall and trellised crops, placing those to the north of the garden or each bed. Document your crops from last season, which may keep growing a few months more, such as garlic or Swiss chard. Remember to keep plant families together as you fill in your beds on paper. Consult companion-planting books for partners in crime. As you assign vegetable locations, move corresponding seed packets out of view, so you know what still needs a space. Make note of what seeds to order and refill. Put the seeds you won't be planting out of view. When you're done, you will have a fully planted plot of land on paper, with perhaps a few empty spaces for whatever tickles your fancy later on.

Congratulations! You're ready to start seeds, prep garden beds, and plant for the season. If you aren't sure where to start, I've provided sample layouts for cool and warm/hot seasons based on my own garden.

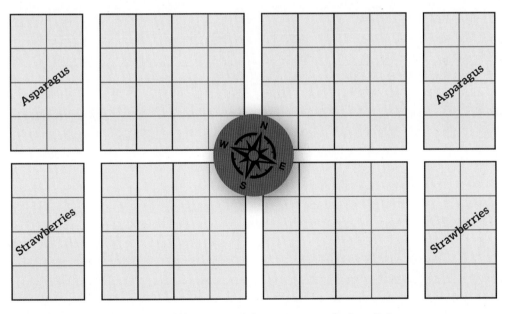

Garden template at Gardenerd HQ: perennial crops are marked, and the open spaces are for annuals.

Asparagus (perennial)

8 Strawberries

15 Potatoes (1 per sq ft)

Garlic (38 using GB on 4" [10cm] centers)

16 Cilantro	16 Cilantro	4 Arugula	4 Arugula
4 Lettuce	4 Lettuce	4 Lettuce	4 Lettuce
4 Lettuce	4 Lettuce	4 Lettuce	4 Lettuce

TRELLIS

8 Snap Peas — 8 Snow Peas

2 Swiss Chard	2 Swiss Chard	2 Swiss Chard	2 Swiss Chard
16 Carrots	16 Carrots	16 Beets	16 Beets
9 Spinach	9 Spinach	9 Spinach

1 Kale	1 Kale	1 Kale	1 Kale
1 Broccoli	1 Broccoli	1 Broccoli	1 Broccoli
1 Cabbage	1 Cabbage	1 Cabbage	1 Cabbage
4 Kohlrabi	4 Kohlrabi	4 Kohlrabi	4 Kohlrabi

Tree Kale (perennial)

8 Strawberries

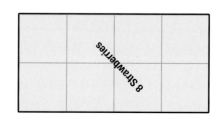

GB = GROW BIOINTENSIVE plant spacing in hexagonal rows

SAMPLE WARM/HOT SEASON LAYOUT

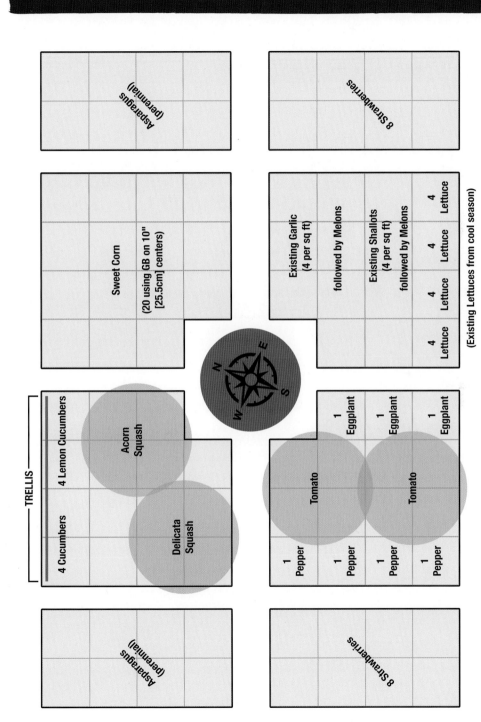

Asparagus (perennial)

8 Strawberries

Sweet Corn

(20 using GB on 10" [25.5cm] centers)

Existing Garlic (4 per sq ft)

followed by Melons

Existing Shallots (4 per sq ft)

followed by Melons

| Lettuce 4 | Lettuce 4 | Lettuce 4 | Lettuce 4 |

(Existing Lettuces from cool season)

TRELLIS

4 Lemon Cucumbers

Acorn Squash

Delicata Squash

4 Cucumbers

| 1 Pepper | 1 Pepper | Tomato | 1 Pepper | 1 Pepper | Tomato |

| 1 Eggplant | 1 Eggplant | 1 Eggplant |

Asparagus (perennial)

8 Strawberries

GB = GROW BIOINTENSIVE plant spacing in hexagonal rows

CHAPTER 5

Small-Space/ Urban Gardening

Unless you live in the wide-open spaces of sun-soaked farmland, chances are you have a limited amount of space available for gardening. Urban gardening keeps growing in popularity (no pun intended), and, more than ever, people are looking for ways to maximize their farmable land. Small-space gardening techniques help you get the most out of your gardening space, whether you have acres or just a balcony.

Start seeds in flats to save space and water during the germination period.

Biointensive Methods

Biointensive is an umbrella term used to describe different gardening methods that help you grow high volumes of produce in small spaces. This chapter will give a brief overview of four biointensive methods that accomplish this task. Some of them focus on true sustainability, incorporating techniques that replenish topsoil, recycle biomass, and build self-sufficient communities. Even if you can't incorporate all of these techniques in total, you can implement some and set goals for others.

Consider Biodynamics

In Chapter 1, we explored the idea that our garden has its own ecosystem by including beneficial flowers, bat houses, and toad abodes. Biodynamics goes a step further and treats the farm or garden itself as a living organism. The principles of biodynamics were founded by Rudolf Steiner (1861–1925) in Europe in the early 1920s. Steiner believed in much more than soil microbiology and the marvel of transpiration in plants. He believed the living organism of a farm goes beyond the boundaries of the farm's fence. It includes the cycle of seasons and, beyond that, even the lunar cycle and other cycles of our solar system. It might sound hokey to some, but there are plenty of successful biodynamic farms, vineyards, and orchards that can attest to the benefits of considering these concepts.

Biodynamics, at its core, is about creating a sustainable organism (your garden) that is as close to self-reliant as possible. The folks at Demeter Association, Inc., the institution that certifies biodynamic farms, have summarized the concept perfectly by saying, "An important social value of biodynamic farming is that it does not depend on the mining of the earth's natural resource base but instead emphasizes contributing to it."

So how does a biodynamic farm work? For starters, it strives to integrate crops and livestock together. Animal manures are wonderful high-nitrogen fertilizers. Farmers use the manures from livestock to feed the crops. The crops feed the livestock in return. It's a closed-loop system. Of course, humans are in there somewhere, helping facilitate the cycle from animals to crops and back. We are also eating the results. You might be asking, "But how does livestock work in a small-space situation?" Let's take a look.

Biodynamic Livestock

While it's not for everyone, if you have room for a few chickens, you have a resource for animal manure to feed to your compost bin. The compost in turn feeds your garden. Chickens also eat grubs from the compost bin and bugs from the garden. If your garden isn't large enough for chickens or livestock of any kind, then look to a friend who might

Chickens can contribute to your ecosystem by eating unwanted insects.

be willing—you can expand that ecosystem to include neighbors with horses, goats, or even rabbits.

As mentioned, biodynamics also uses the lunar calendar to determine favorable days for planting, harvesting, and starting seeds. *Stella Natura* (stellanatura.com), the yearly publication that tracks the phases of the moon and its subsequent gravitational pull, is the tool by which most biodynamic farmers live and plant. There is science to support this stuff. In a 10-year study, Dr. Frank A. Brown showed that plants absorbed more water during full moons. Other research has shown that seeds germinate more quickly if planted two days before the new moon. Whether you believe in it or not, the idea behind biodynamics is to use all environmental observations (and influences) to create a healthy, productive, and sustainable operation.

Along with sustainable practices, biodynamics encourages the use of specific preparations (numbered 500–508) to inoculate compost piles, strengthen microbial life, and prevent diseases. These preparations include key herbs like valerian, stinging nettle, chamomile, and yarrow. They are grown on the farm and fermented into a compost-like consistency or liquid that is then combined with or sprayed onto compost piles.

You may be wondering how all of this applies to small spaces. Hold tight—it will all become clear shortly. For now, just remember the key points about biodynamics: the

GARDENING TIP:
THE SCIENCE OF COMPOSTING

A study was conducted at Washington State University's Department of Soil Sciences using compost piles of cow manure and wood shavings. Biodynamic preparations were applied to some of the piles, but not to the control piles. The same amount of water was used in each pile.

After eight weeks of active composting, "biodynamic-treated composts maintained an average 3.4°C [6°F] higher temperature . . . suggesting more thermophilic microbial activity and/or faster development of compost with BD treatment. . . . At the final sampling, BD-treated piles respired CO_2 at a 10 percent lower rate and had a larger ratio of dehydrogenase enzyme activity to CO_2 production . . . Final samples of BD-treated compost also had 65 percent more nitrate than control piles. Biodynamic preparations thus effected discernible change in compost chemical and microbial parameters." How's that for an ecosystem!

farm as a living organism, the integration of crops and livestock, and the recycling of nutrients (composting).

What Is French Intensive?

Prior to the twentieth century, just outside Paris, farmers grew food using a method that conserved space and resources. They recycled horse manure from the transportation department and turned it into fecund soil that yielded plentiful crops—far more than traditional row farms produced. They carried the manure in baskets that were worn like backpacks, with long boards extending overhead to keep tall

This biointensively planted garlic takes up 8 sq ft (0.7 sq m) and will last up to nine months in storage.

mounds of manure from falling onto their heads. Like biodynamics, French intensive gardening has its own set of principles that governed the way land was cultivated and crops were raised.

Soil Depth

French intensive farmers conditioned their soil to a depth of 24" (61cm) using a technique called double digging (see Part 2 for a tutorial). Preparing the soil to that depth allowed plants to develop stronger and deeper root systems, enabling them to pull nutrients and minerals from otherwise inaccessible soils below.

Raised Beds

These were not necessarily traditional wooden raised beds, although vintage photos have shown them in use. Typically, mounded raised beds were a result of double digging. After working in compost or manure to condition the soil, the beds were naturally elevated. Farmers were careful not to step on the beds once prepared. Beds/mounds were usually 5' (1.5m) wide but could be as long as 100' (30.5m).

Hexagonal Planting

Also known as offset rows or diagonal planting, this method allows farmers to plant more seedlings in each bed. The plants are placed in an offset pattern rather than in traditional rows with pathways between each row.

What does hexagonal planting look like? Let's say you have a sheet of chicken wire. Lay it down on the soil, place a bean seed in the center of each hole in the wire mesh,

5" (13cm) centers—5" (13cm) apart in all directions

Hexagonal spacing is a key component of the French Intensive method.

and then lift up the chicken wire. Each seed will be equidistant from every other seed on all sides. Your first row of seeds will be a straight line across the top. Your second row of seeds will start below the first, exactly halfway between the first and second seed of the first row. What are the benefits of hexagonal planting? There are many.

1. By planting hexagonally, plants are closer together than they would be in traditional rows, which means you can fit more into the same amount of space.
2. As plants grow, their shoulders touch, creating a living mulch. This eliminates sun and heat, greatly reducing weeds and evaporation of precious water.
3. Just like the penguins at the South Pole, huddling together for warmth, plants grown hexagonally create a microclimate for themselves, which supports healthy crops. French intensive farmers often protected young plants with individual cloches (glass bells) to create a mini-greenhouse for each plant. See Part 2 to learn how to make your own.

Succession Planting

French intensive farmers planted their beds over time, rather than all at once, to maintain a steady harvest throughout the season. If you love lettuce but don't want 20 heads of romaine all at once, you can do what these farmers did: Plant a 1'–2' (30.5–61cm) section of a raised bed with lettuce seeds or transplants (hexagonally, of course) on day one. On day 14, plant another 2' (61cm). Repeat until you run out of space for lettuce, and you'll never run out of lettuce.

As another type of succession planting, farmers planted short-season crops immediately following long-season crops in order to have something growing in the garden at all times. They never left soil bare and, as a result, achieved upward of nine crops per season from the same plot of land.

Start seeds throughout the growing season to keep your garden beds full and productive.

These beds are biointensively planted with (left to right) asparagus, sweet corn, and garbanzo beans.

GROW BIOINTENSIVE® (Mini-Farming)

Biodynamics and French intensive gardening can be applied to small spaces to get the most out of your garden. Let's look at how these two techniques were combined to form a newer biointensive growing method that is used by millions today.

Alan Chadwick, an Englishman born in 1909, is credited for taking the key principles of biodynamics and French intensive methods and combining them into something new. He mentored with Steiner and, some 40 years later in 1967, started the University of California (UC) Santa Cruz Garden Project. He developed an agricultural technique that combined double digging and hexagonal planting from the French intensive method with the farm-as-living-organism, lunar calendar, and crop/livestock integration principles from biodynamics.

John Jeavons furthered Chadwick's work with another 50 years of research to develop what is now widely known as GROW BIOINTENSIVE®, or mini-farming. His research is published in his book *How to Grow More Vegetables*. The basis for Jeavons's research came from the realization that our planet is losing farmable land due to soil erosion and desertification, caused by unsustainable farming practices and the destruction of rainforests. For every pound (450g) of conventionally grown food we consume, Jeavons says between 6–24 pounds (2.75–11kg) of viable topsoil are lost. Organic farming is better but still not sustainable. For every pound (450g) of organically grown food we consume, 3–5 pounds (1.5–2.25kg) of viable topsoil are lost.

We currently require between 7,000 and 63,000 sq ft (650 and 5,853 sq m) of land per person (less for a vegan lifestyle; more for a high-animal-product diet) to grow every bit of food as well as materials for clothing, fuel, and shelter. Our population is growing, leaving less land per person. Jeavons's research shows that we can count on having fewer than 9,000 sq ft (836 sq m) of viable farmland per person in the near future to fulfill our essential needs. If that's the outlook of the future, then logically we would need to be as efficient as possible with our land, right?

Jeavons set out to find a way to use less land while creating a system that affords people who have few or no resources—water, fertilizer, land, and money—a sustainable way to grow high-calorie crops and a means to earn income. GROW BIOINTENSIVE was born, using double digging, hexagonal planting, recycling of nutrients, and more to reduce the amount of land needed per person to only 4,000 sq ft (372 sq m).

Whether you have 4,000 or 400 sq ft (372 or 37 sq m) to work with, you can apply these practices for a more sustainable garden. There are a few key components to GROW BIOINTENSIVE worth noting. We've already covered double digging for soil conditioning and hexagonal planting for efficient plant spacing, but let's look at another important principle to consider. It's a magic formula for sustainability: 60:30:10. What does it mean?

Sixty Percent

Remember how we talked about inputs and having to go to the nursery to buy bagged soil and fertilizer for the garden? What if you never had to do that? What if you were able to grow enough nitrogen- and carbon-rich material on your land so that, at the end of the season, you could cut it all down and put it in your compost bin; and, a few months later, you would have enough high-quality compost to feed your garden and rejuvenate those beds? That would be great. That would be a closed-loop system. These nitrogen- and carbon-rich materials are called carbon and calorie crops. Corn and other grains, such as wheat, rye, barley, millet, quinoa, amaranth, and oats, are all great sources of biomass for the compost bin, but they also give you a harvest before cutting down the material. Fava beans are also on the list. These crops serve the dual purpose of providing calories and biomass.

So what's this 60 percent all about? Think of it as a goal. It may take a while for you to attain it, but if you can dedicate 60 percent of your garden space to growing these carbon and calorie crops, you will have enough material to generate enough compost to feed your garden all year, without trips to the nursery. If 60 percent sounds like too much, start with 25 percent—one raised bed out of four each season. You'll see the difference it makes in the quality of your compost and the contents of your wallet.

Thirty Percent

If you lived in a country where food was scarce and land was precious, it would be advantageous to grow crops that provided the highest calorie content per square foot as possible. Crops like potatoes, parsnips, and sweet potatoes provide a lot of calories, but, more importantly, they provide higher yields (calories included) per square foot. The 30 percent part of the equation is relegated to these crops. If you can dedicate 30 percent of your land to growing high-calorie crops, you can feed your family more substantially with less land.

Ten Percent

The remaining 10 percent is for all the crops you love to grow, like tomatoes, peppers, squashes, lettuces, and carrots. It might sound a little depressing to think that such a small amount of land is dedicated to the crops we're used to growing, but, in truth, those other crops aren't wasted, either. They help provide sustenance for your family and food for your compost bin.

A GROW BIOINTENSIVE garden might have corn and quinoa growing in the spring/summer, followed by fava beans or another cover crop over winter. It might also have potatoes and sunflowers (grown for the nutritious seeds and biomass), parsnips, and Jerusalem artichokes—another 30 percent crop. Then, there might be a section of broccolis, carrots, lettuces, and peas. It doesn't sound too far off from a traditional garden. The difference is that these crops are planted hexagonally in deeply conditioned soil, using companion planting and crop rotation, and the compost made

Potatoes are a 30 percent crop because they provide high calories and take less space to grow.

The Square-Foot Gardening method creates an orderly "patchwork quilt" of vegetables in your garden beds.

from the biomass is going to feed the garden more effectively, instead of eroding soil away with conventional methods.

There is much, much more to the GROW BIOINTENSIVE method. If you are interested in learning more, check out *How to Grow More Vegetables* or the abridged publication by John Jeavons and Carol Cox, *The Sustainable Vegetable Garden*.

Square-Foot Gardening

There is one more biointensive method to discuss, and it is one that was created with science-minded gardeners in mind. It was invented by an engineer named Mel Bartholomew. Back in the 1980s, he was searching for a better way to garden. He wanted to reduce the space needed to grow food, decrease water, and eliminate as much labor as possible. As engineers often do, he questioned everything. In particular, he questioned traditional row farming. After a successful television series on PBS and a book outlining all the details of his innovative method, millions of gardeners have adopted his way of doing things.

Square-foot gardening, as the name implies, is based on using square feet instead of rows to plot out crops. Based on a 4' x 4' (1.2 x 1.2m) raised bed, Bartholomew claimed that you could grow a laundry list of vegetables in one bed, including a head each of broccoli, cauliflower, and cabbage; 16 heads of lettuce; 5 pounds (2.25kg) of peas; 16 scallions; 32 carrots; 32 beets (with greens); 32 radishes; 8 Swiss chard plants; 9 spinach plants, and 9 turnips. Sound impossible? Not so.

Bartholomew's method divides square feet equally into sections, like a four square court or tic-tac-toe board, depending on how far apart plants need to be spaced. If

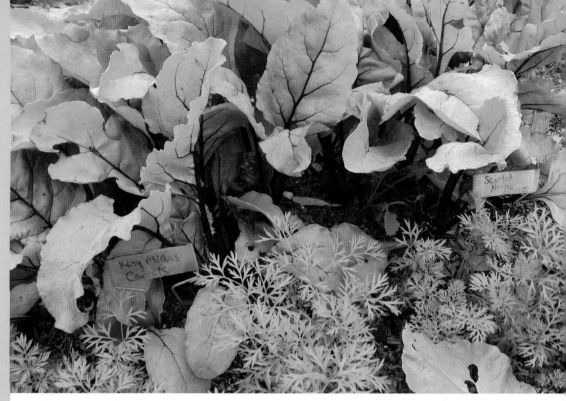

These beets and carrots were planted using square-foot gardening spacing techniques (without physical grids, which Bartholomew insists on using for true square-foot gardening.

plants need to be 12" (30.5cm) apart at maturity, plant one in the center of each square foot and—*poof!* Those plants are 12" (30.5cm) apart. Vegetables like lettuces generally need to be 6" (15cm) apart. By dividing a square foot into four quarters and planting one lettuce in the center of each quarter, those lettuces are all 6" (15cm) apart from each other. That's four lettuces per square foot. If you have only a balcony, using this method you can grow enough salad greens in 2 sq ft (0.2 sq m) to make salads for one person for three months. Just harvest the outside leaves, and those eight heads of lettuce will keep producing all season long.

Much like other biointensive methods, Bartholomew's technique of planting vegetables close together creates that living mulch we talked about earlier. Plant shoulders touch, blocking out the sun, keeping soil moist and weed-free. That equals less labor and water, and more food for gardeners.

The strategy behind using raised beds no larger than 4' x 4' (1.2 x 1.2m) is simple. An adult can reach about 2' (61cm) into a garden without stepping on the soil. If you have access on all four sides, you will be able to access the entire raised bed easily. If you situate your bed up against the wall, the bed should be narrower to accommodate having access on only three sides, even less if access is available on only one side.

By dividing the 4' x 4' (1.2 x 1.2m) raised bed into 16 equal squares, Bartholomew discovered that each square could be worked individually. For example, let's say we have radishes planted in one square and lettuces in a second square next to it. Radishes sprout and grow quickly and will be ready to harvest long before the lettuces. According to Bartholomew, you can harvest those radishes and then use a hand trowel to add a handful of compost to that now-empty square. It's now ready to plant again without ever disturbing the lettuces next door. In fact, after initial setup, you can work your garden without ever using a shovel again.

Square-foot gardening has its own method of starting seeds, as well as plenty of shortcuts to reduce waste, including seeds. There is also a patented soil formula for those interested in square-foot gardening; while there is no "perfect" soil formula, see page 212 for a variation on this formula. Traditional farming (and instructions on every seed packet) will have you sprinkling seeds in a row, backfilling the soil to cover the seeds, watering the entire row, and waiting for the seeds to sprout. Once they do, you have to go back and thin the rows—pull or cut out any sprout that is not a certain distance from its neighbor. What a waste of seeds, time, and energy. Bartholomew's method has you drilling holes exactly where the seeds are going to grow to maturity. You drop in a seed or two, cover them up, and water one square foot instead of a long row. A germination test (see the sidebar on page 223) will help determine seed viability, so you won't waste time planting seeds that won't germinate.

Bartholomew developed a scientific way to plant seeds. It goes like this: use your finger to drill a hole for your crop according to his grid-pattern method (one, four, nine, or sixteen holes per square foot), drop in a seed, and backfill the hole. What makes this technique cool is that you know exactly where your seeds are planted, and you know exactly where to water. Not only that—you will know exactly where to replant if your seeds don't emerge.

The great thing about square-foot gardening is that it's malleable. You can adapt it to any size or space. Make L shapes in corners, long and narrow planters along side yards, or a child's garden with smaller raised beds. Square-foot gardening advises ways to modify raised beds for concrete patios or elevate them for those in wheelchairs. It also maintains that you can save space by growing up instead of out.

Vertical gardening has become more popular in recent years, but Bartholomew has been preaching the benefits of growing crops up trellises long before it was hip to plant a living roof or wall. Sure, we're accustomed to seeing crops like cucumbers and pole beans winding up a trellis, but what about cantaloupes or butternut squash? It's possible with square-foot gardening. Here's a chance to use that ratty old T-shirt or those pantyhose with an unsightly run. As fruit develops, you can fashion a sling from the sleeves of dad's old sweatshirt and tie it securely to the trellis. Melons ripen without pulling down the vines because they are fully supported.

***

Pumpkins and other squashes can be candidates for vertical gardening.

While you can use each of these biointensive methods individually, adventurous gardeners can combine the techniques to see just how efficient their gardens can be. Try hexagonal spacing and vertical gardening together. Play with double digging and formal raised beds to see if you can improve yields. These techniques came about from years of trial and error and, finally, success. You may come up with the next best biointensive method yet.

Manipulating Sunlight

Small-space gardeners are often faced with more than just space constraints. Apartment and condo dwellers also deal with sun exposure, or the lack thereof. With people stacked on top of one another in urban communities, it can be difficult to find a spot that has full sun—for at least six hours of sunlight each day. One solution is to head to the roof, but if that's not an option, what else can you do?

Get Some Wheels

Plant in containers that are outfitted with casters so you can roll the pots to the sunny parts of the balcony, patio, or yard as needed. This way, you can gain several hours of sunlight.

Elevate

Sometimes a little height can do wonders. Here's an example: A woman had a corner garden plot that would get decent sun were it not in the shadow of an annoying staircase that blocked light from ever touching the soil. She found an old cane chair with a broken seat and relocated a pot to fit snugly in the seat of the chair. She did something similar with other pots. By elevating her containers just a couple of feet (30–60cm), they were now tall enough to reach sunlight. The plants thrived and climbed up the staircase railing to the second floor.

Reflect

Whiteboards are widely used in the film and television industry to bounce light into dark corners. They work for gardens, too. A word of warning though: stick to just whiteboards rather than mirrors or other focused light reflectors. The point is not to fry your plants, just to extend their exposure to light.

Add a Grow Light

If you are gardening up against a wall with access to electricity, you can install a powerful grow light (like the kind used in greenhouses or hydroponics) with full-spectrum light bulbs to extend daylight exposure. Some high-powered lights require a ballast to prevent flickering or power surges. Generally speaking, grow lights work best when they are within 3" (7.5cm) of plant surfaces, so this may not be an option for gardens of varying sizes.

Grow lights make starting seeds indoors easier, and they help produce stocky, sturdier plants.

No Space?

There are other options to try if your garden space isn't much of a garden space. Yard-sharing organizations such as Shared Earth (*sharedearth.com*) in the United States and Lend and Tend in the United Kingdom (*lendandtend.com*) match up people who want to garden with people who have yards they don't want to tend. Join a community garden (or get on the waiting list for one) and enjoy your own plot of land for a yearly fee. Don't know of any gardens near you? You can search for one on the American Community Garden Association's website (*communitygarden.org*). Just plug in your zip code and see what secret gardens await you.

CHAPTER 6

Planting Nitty-Gritty

OK, you've done your garden bed prep, you've planned out your growing space, and you've chosen what to grow based on your hardiness zone and frost dates. Now it's time to get down to the nitty-gritty and plant something. In this chapter, you will learn what to do with all those seeds and transplants from the nursery. We'll cover step-by-step instructions for planting as well as how to grow specific vegetables each season. You'll learn about the difference between heirloom and open-pollinated seeds, between hybrids and GMOs. You'll even find out how to choose a good plant from the nursery if you decide not to grow from seed.

How to Plant from Seed

When you're ready to plant, remove your seeds from the fridge (see Seed Storage the Gardenerd Way in Part 2), grab your garden plan, and head for the great outdoors. If you know exactly what you're going to plant, you might want to take those seeds out of the jar and keep them in your pocket. If the whole jar is making the trip to the garden, make sure to set it down in a shady place, out of direct sunlight.

There are several ways to plant seeds. Most seed packets will offer plenty of advice about how deep to plant and how far apart. If you've misplaced your seed packet, see the sidebar about seed depth (see opposite page) for help.

If you are using a biointensive method of planting, measure the distance between your plants based on the "space after thinning" dimensions on the seed packet and mark the soil. If you are drilling holes with your finger, here's a useful trick: wet your planting area first. Dry soil will not hold a shape when you drill a planting hole; it will just collapse in on itself. Save time by watering the soil just a bit. You don't want to soak it, but just give it enough moisture to hold together without collapsing.

Chard seeds are really clusters of seeds. More than one seed germinates from each other.

If you want to plant in rows, use the edge of your hand or a hand trowel to cut a shallow trench into the soil. Some gardeners prefer to use a hoe for the task. It's all good. Just remember that seeds aren't planted very deep. If you get too enthusiastic, your ½" (1.25cm) deep trench will be 2½" (6.5cm) deep. For those with perfectionist tendencies, lay a rake handle down and press it into the soil for a perfect line. Lift the rake, distribute your seeds, and backfill the soil into place.

To prevent dumping all your seeds out onto the soil at once, take your gloves off and pour a small number of seeds into your nondominant hand. Use the thumb and index finger of your dominant hand to swizzle a seed or two into each planting hole or along a trench. Return the unused seeds to the packet by holding the seed packet by the outer edges and squeezing the packet so it opens like a mouth. Cup the hand with the seeds and tip the seeds back into the packet. It's not rocket science, but you'd be surprised how many people have trouble getting those little buggers back to safety.

How to Plant from Nursery Stock

Transplants, or starts, from nurseries can save time and prevent failures for new gardeners. Local garden centers sell tried-and-true varieties that are nearly guaranteed to grow in your hardiness zone. You can pick up a 4" (10cm) pot or six-pack of lettuces over the weekend and be harvesting outer leaves a month later. Essentially, nursery stock saves you about six weeks compared to growing from seed. The downside of buying nursery stock is you are limited to what the nursery has on hand. That said, the array of available heirlooms and more unusual varieties is broadening each year as gardeners demand them.

These nursery seedlings are ready to plant.

While most nurseries keep their selections fresh, some less reputable garden centers continue to sell transplants that are past their prime. Unsuspecting new gardeners wouldn't know any better, so the following tips will guide you in how to pick good plants from the nursery.

Choose Small, Stout Plants

Remember that a plant has foliage above and roots below. Plant roots go down (or they would, if they had room) as far as the foliage reaches upward. So if you see a plant in a 4" (10cm) pot with a foot or two (30–60cm) of foliage above the soil level, pass on it. Opt for stocky plants that are just getting their start. If the ratio of roots to foliage is more equal, those plants will thrive when transplanted.

Sometimes you will find a plant that has a spindly stem with a lot of distance between leaf sets. That's a leggy plant. Leggy plants didn't get enough sun and are not good candidates for your garden. Resist the urge to rescue the underdog; choose the stocky plant instead.

Watch Out for Diseases

A few yellow leaves here and there aren't a bad thing, but if you see signs of powdery mildew or blight on a plant, don't take it home. Withered leaves, brown splotches, and fuzzy white patches on leaves are sure signs of disease. Because the whole point of starting with transplants is to increase your success rate and shorten your growing time, start with healthy plants.

Avoid Flowers or Fruit

It's so tempting to buy a vegetable start that is already flowering or setting fruit. The hard work is already done for you, right? Not quite. Once a plant starts to produce fruit, the plant's focus is no longer on root development. When you buy a seedling, you want the plant to focus on root development first, flowering and fruiting later. If you do find yourself having to choose from veggie plants with flowers or fruit, pinch them off to refocus the plant's energy on root production. You'll end up with a higher-yielding plant in the long run.

Plant Properly

Once you've chosen your nursery stock, it's important to plant them properly. Sure, you could just pull them out of their pots and plop them in the soil, but you'll give your plants a fighting chance if you take an extra step or two.

First, water the transplants well. Some gardeners like to submerge the pots in a bucket of water just above the soil level until air bubbles stop rising. A good drenching will accomplish the same thing. Next, dig your planting hole just as deep as your pot. You can set the transplant into the planting hole while it's still in the pot to see if the soil levels align. Not deep enough? Lift out the plant and keep digging. Some plants, such as tomatoes, can be buried deeper than the existing soil level, but most plants prefer to be installed at the same level.

Throw a handful of fertilizer into the hole and scratch it in with your fingers. Mix it in well to avoid direct contact with plant roots. (**Note:** If you have amended your beds before planting, this step is not necessary.) Squeeze the pot around the sides to loosen the soil and more easily remove the root ball.

Place your thumb and forefinger (or do the Spock "live long and prosper" thing if you want) on either side of the plant stem, covering the soil with your hand, and then flip the plant upside-down so the root ball is facing up and the foliage is facing down. Pull off the pot.

Now comes the part that many gardeners leave out. Take the bottom of the root ball in your hands and tease the roots apart with your fingers. Just pull the soil and roots apart a little bit to open them up and give them guidance—you're pointing them in a new direction. Some gardeners use scissors to trim the roots to trigger a new growth process. It isn't necessary, but if you feel compelled, go ahead and give it a try. Now your plant is ready to go into the ground.

Set the plant upright in the planting hole and gently backfill the soil around it. Be careful not to compact the soil. Instead, leave it loose and let water do the job for you. By watering the soil immediately afterward, it naturally removes air pockets and settles the soil around your plants. You may need to add more soil to fill in sunken spots, but that's better than to have squeezed all the air out of your soil.

To help plants recover from possible transplant shock, which can make them wilt or suffer a setback within a week or two after planting, water newly transplanted crops with a mixture of water and kelp emulsion. As mentioned earlier, kelp emulsion or liquid kelp extract contains a broad spectrum of minerals and naturally occurring growth hormones that help ease plants into their new homes.

Proper care of your plants will create a lush garden you want to show off.

ALL ABOUT SEEDS: HEIRLOOM, OPEN-POLLINATED, AND HYBRID SEEDS

When you're ready to dive into planting your garden from seeds rather than transplants, there are a few things to know about seeds before you amass your collection. Seeds embody history. They contain stories from past generations and tell us about the climates and conditions they have adapted to over the centuries. There are seeds that have naturally cross-pollinated over generations to become stronger and well adapted to certain climates. Then there are new seeds, developed by careful hybridization, which feature desirable traits like deeper colors, larger fruit, or stronger disease resistance. Let's talk about these individually.

- **Heirloom**—Anything that has been handed down from generation to generation is considered an heirloom. While some antique dealers say an heirloom must be at least 100 years old, there is no specific time frame associated with heirloom seeds. The general consensus, however, is that seeds found in existence prior to the 1950s can be called heirlooms. Why the 1950s? Because that's when the first hybrid seeds were put into commercial production (even though some sources say hybrids were used as far back as the 1930s). An heirloom is an open-pollinated seed (we'll talk about that next) that was not used in commercial agriculture. Heirloom varieties are often regional or rare. Once you start growing heirlooms, you'll never be satisfied with boring old market-variety produce again.

- **Open-pollinated**—These plants are the result of cross-pollinating via the wind, birds, or bees. Seeds saved from these plants will produce plants just like their parents. In other words, they breed "true to type." If you plant the seeds that were saved from an open-pollinated plant, the resulting plant will look and taste just like its parent. Theoretically, as you save seeds year after year from plants that thrived in your garden, those seeds will produce stronger, well-adapted plants for your climate. Just keep this part straight: an heirloom is open-pollinated, but not all open-pollinated seeds are heirlooms. Both types of seeds are exactly what you want to have on hand for survival when the zombie apocalypse strikes.

- **Hybrid**—A hybrid seed is produced with human intervention by crossing two different parent plants, usually from the same species. Because this generally occurs in a controlled environment, nature can't reproduce it, so the process must be duplicated each year by breeders in order to achieve the same results. In other words, seeds saved from hybridized plants don't breed true to type. They are wild cards. They will revert to some other part of their genetics and are therefore not reliable for seed saving.

- **GMOs**—Let's not confuse hybrids with genetically modified organisms (GMOs) or genetically engineered (GE) seeds. Hybridization occurs under controlled conditions, but genetic modification occurs under a microscope. Strands of DNA are cut and spliced, replacing part of the vegetable's natural genetic makeup with something from another organism. Like an organ transplant process, the organism can reject the transplant (in this case, the foreign DNA), so biotechnologists use what's

Dragon tongue beans are a beautiful heirloom addition to any garden.

called a viral promoter to ensure that the new DNA takes. Virtually every GMO out there was created by inserting the cauliflower mosaic virus into the DNA strands. There's a plethora of disconcerting information about this fact, and if you want to read more, start with the Non-GMO Project (*nongmoproject.org*).

Examples of GMO technology: GMO corn has been altered to produce its own pesticides. Soybean crops have been modified to withstand constant applications of systemic weed killers. While the debate goes on about whether GMO foods are safe to consume, the organic industry is steering clear of them. So, at this time, if you buy organic seeds or produce, they are GMO-free (barring the ever-increasing cross-contamination from wind–pollinated GMO crops). At the time of this printing, there is one GMO purple tomato seed available to home gardeners, but more may become available. Look for seed catalogs from companies that subscribe to the Safe Seed Pledge, which states that the company does not knowingly or willingly grow or sell GMO seeds. Flip to Part 2 to find a list of trusted seed companies as well as great heirloom/open-pollinated seeds to try.

VEGETABLE PROFILES

Now that you have the basics of how to plant from seed and from nursery stock, it's a good time to talk about specific plants. This section profiles an array of easy-to-grow vegetables (followed by a section on herbs) that are suitable for small-space gardeners and beginners as well as veteran green thumbs. As you grow your garden, use these plant profiles to help guide your way through the season. **Note:** Plant spacing is based on biointensive methods. Those using row-farming techniques would space plants farther apart than what is suggested here.

Most annual vegetables will grow well in hardiness zones 3–11, but perennial and overwintering vegetable crops may need protection or relocation indoors over winter in cold-winter climates. You will also find the preferred soil pH for each crop listed in these plant profiles, but again, don't let it deter you if your soil pH is different.

Take advantage of your small-space garden by growing a variety of veggies.

Arugula

Arugula

Latin name: *Eruca vesicaria* or *Eruca sativa*
Seed planting depth: ¼"–½" (0.5–1.25cm)
Plant spacing: 4"–6" (10–15cm)
Soil temperature for germination:
45°F–70°F (7°C–21°C)
Sun: Full to partial
Water: Moderate
Days to germinate: 3 to 7
Days to maturity: 25 to 45
Preferred soil pH: 6.0–8.0

About Arugula

Arugula is an annual (see Glossary) plant native to the Mediterranean and has been grown since Roman times, both in the wild and in commercial agriculture. Its leaves are peppery and look similar to radish leaves. The leaves, blossoms, seed pods, and mature seeds of the plant are all edible. Though typically used raw in salads to add a spicy punch to other greens, it can also be cooked with pasta or meats or pureed into a sauce. In traditional southern European dishes, the leaves are also used on pizzas and in pesto.

Growing Arugula

Arugula seed is best sown directly into the garden where you intend to grow it to maturity. Plant the seeds 4"–6" (10–15cm) apart. Gently cover them with ¼" (0.5cm) of soil and water. Arugula prefers a cool soil temperature and tends to bolt to seed in summer heat and dry inland areas, so grow it in the fall/winter and spring seasons. Plant in fertile, loose soil. Water every day until the seeds germinate and then water them as needed to keep the soil moist but not soggy.

Harvesting Arugula

The seeds should sprout in three to seven days (slightly longer in cooler temperatures). For a continuous crop, sow more seeds every two weeks to ensure that new cuttings are available at regular intervals. Arugula matures very quickly—typically within 40 days—so get ready to start harvesting in as little as four weeks. Harvest the outside leaves while they are young and tender. The larger arugula gets, the more pungent it becomes. Allow the hardiest plants to bolt to seed and set flowers. When the pods become dry and brittle, carefully remove them from the plant and crush them over a bowl. You will find six to eight seeds in each pod. Place them in a labeled envelope or plastic bag to keep for future use. At the end of the season, pull and compost any remaining plants and roots.

Beans

Latin name: *Phaseolus vulgaris*
Planting depth: ¾"–1½" (2–3.75cm)
Plant spacing: 4"–6" (10–15cm)
Soil temperature for germination:
    70°F–85°F (21°C–29°C)
Sun: Full
Water: Moderate
Days to germinate: 6 to 12
Days to maturity: 55 to 60
Preferred soil pH: 6.0–7.5

About Beans

Beans are available as bush or pole varieties and yield well, requiring very little work. If you have limited trellis space, opt for bush beans, because they don't require trellising. Pole beans need support but provide multiple harvests if allowed to grow as perennials.

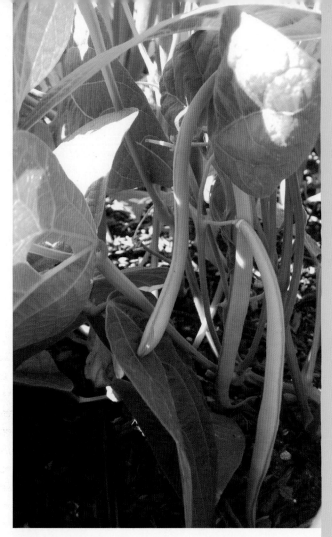

Bush green beans

Growing Beans

Beans should be planted after threat of frost is passed. Plant seeds about 1" (2.5cm) deep, about 4" (10cm) apart for bush varieties and 6" (15cm) apart for pole beans. Soak bean seeds before planting (but no longer than four hours, or they might rot) and coat them with a bean inoculant to increase germination success. Keep the seed bed moist until germination occurs. Water them regularly thereafter. For a continuous supply of snap beans through spring and summer, plant more seeds every two to four weeks until early August.

Harvesting Beans

Beans can be harvested fresh or left to dry on the vine for soup/dry beans. For fresh beans, choose pods that are firm, but pick them before the seeds within the pods have filled out, as they will be more tender. Wait until morning dew has dried before picking to prevent the spread of bean bacterial blight. Hold the stem with one hand and pull the pods with the other to prevent breaking the tender shoots. Plants will form new flowers and pods if you harvest regularly before the seeds mature.

Common Problems

Bean mosaic diseases appear as distorted, yellowish-green mottled leaves and inhibit the production of pods. If you notice this in your garden, switch to a mosaic-resistant bean variety. Bacterial bean blight is another culprit. Bright yellow or brown spots on the leaves or water-soaked spots on the pods indicate the presence of the disease. It is a seed-borne disease, so start with disease-free seed and don't touch the plant while it's wet (the disease can spread that way). Don't compost the waste unless your compost pile reaches at least 130°F (54.5°C).

For those with small spaces, growing vertically might be the perfect solution. Pole beans just need a trellis or other support.

Beets

Beets

Latin name: *Beta vulgaris*

Planting depth: ½"–1" (1.25–2.5cm)

Plant spacing: 3" (7.5cm)

Soil temperature to germination:
55°F–75°F (13°C–24°C)

Sun: Full to partial

Water: Moderate

Days to germinate: 5 to 10

Days to maturity: 55 to 70

Preferred soil pH: 6.0–7.5

About Beets

Beets are sweet, nutritious, and easy to grow in just about any conditions. They are available to grow in different varieties, offering a rainbow of colors and shapes: red, purple, gold, or white; round, oval, or cylindrical. Both the roots and the leaves are edible. If your weather is severe, look for cultivars that tolerate extreme temperatures. To stock your root cellar, look for beets with good keeping qualities.

Growing Beets

Beets are best sown directly into the soil where you intend to grow them to maturity. Plant beets in early spring (or fall in warm-winter climates). Plant seeds 3" (7.5cm) apart and ½"–1" (1.25–2.5cm) deep. For an ongoing harvest of tender roots, plant seeds every 20 to 30 days from early spring through mid-summer. Plan to plant your last beet about four to seven weeks before the first expected frost date.

Beets perform best in full sun but tolerate partial shade too. They love water, so keep the soil moist. They can withstand freezing temperatures, but young plants exposed to two to three weeks of temperatures below 50°F (10°C) may go to seed prematurely. Most beet seeds produce a cluster of sprouts, so you'll want to thin them with scissors when they emerge.

Harvesting Beets

Beets can be harvested between 50 and 70 days after sowing seeds. For baby beets, harvest sooner. Beet greens are ready to harvest in just 30 to 45 days. Pull up roots when they are 1½"–3" (3.75–7.5cm) wide. You can check the size by running a finger around the shoulder of the root. Lift roots out of the soil carefully to avoid bruising them. Remove any dirt and then cut the tops off, leaving at least 1" (2.5cm) of the stem to prevent the roots from bleeding. They can be refrigerated for several weeks or layered in a box filled with sand or peat and stored in a cool spot for two to five months. Beets can be frozen, canned, or pickled.

Loosen the soil around the beet before carefully pulling it out of the ground.

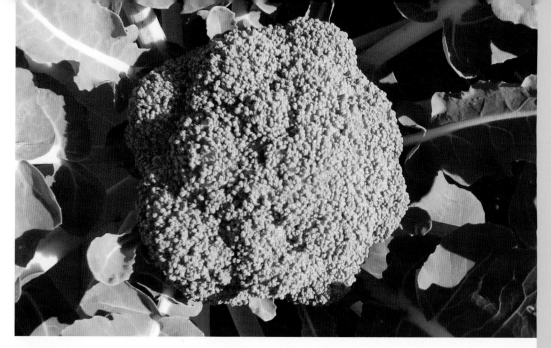

Broccoli

Broccoli

Latin name: *Brassica oleracea* var. *italica*
Planting depth: ¼"–½" (0.5–1.25cm)
Plant spacing: 12" (30.5cm) apart
Soil temperature for germination: 55°F–85°F (13°C–29.5°C)
Sun: Full
Water: Moderate
Days to germinate: 5 to 14
Days to maturity: 60 to 90
Preferred soil pH: 6.0–7.0

About Broccoli

Broccoli is a hardy cole crop that is high in vitamins A and D and is best grown during the cooler seasons of the year. Broccoli evolved from a wild cabbage plant in Europe as early as the sixth century BCE. Since the Roman Empire, broccoli has been considered a uniquely valuable food among Italians. However, it was not until the 1920s that broccoli became a regular dinner feature in the United States.

Growing Broccoli

Broccoli plants of most varieties can produce a harvest over an entire season if grown properly. Once the center head is harvested, side shoots continue to produce, extending the harvest over several months. In most parts of the country, it is possible to grow two crops per year. For beginning gardeners, transplants are recommended rather than starting from seed, because broccoli can take a while to develop. However, fall crops are OK to direct-seed in your garden.

Plant one seed or transplant per square foot (0.1 sq m)—or plant a few seeds and then thin. Broccoli plants grow upright with large leaves up to 2½" (6.5cm) tall. For spring planting, start seedlings in mid-winter for transplanting into the garden. Be sure that all threat of frost has passed before planting out. Water well and fertilize the plants mid-season to encourage heads to form.

Harvesting Broccoli

Broccoli heads and stems are edible. A large central head will form first; after that is harvested, smaller side shoots will appear. Cut the central head with 5"–6" (13–15cm) of stem, when the head is tight with buds and fully developed. If you wait too long, the buds start to loosen and separate, and the individual bright yellow flowers start to open. You can still eat it at this point, but it's just not as pretty. Continue harvesting broccoli side shoots for several weeks afterward.

Common Problems

Cabbage worms and aphids are the biggest problem with most brassicas, but the harlequin bug (*Murgantia histronica*) and bagrada bug (*Bagrada hilaris*) can be problems too. Check your brassicas for insects daily—scan the underside of leaves and remove the insects. Use floating row cover (or garden fabric) to prevent cabbage moths from laying eggs on leaves. Keep an eye out for maggots on the stems and roots. Clubroot disease is common in cauliflower, cabbage, broccoli, and so forth if crops are not regularly rotated. Roots swell, or form "clubs," and interfere with the plant's ability to take up food from the soil. Regular crop rotation will help prevent this disease.

Harvest the head of broccoli, but leave the plant intact so it can produce side shoots for weeks to come.

Cabbage

Latin name: *Brassica oleracea* var. *capitate*
Planting depth: ⅜"–½" (1–1.25cm)
Plant spacing: 12" (30.5cm)
Soil temperature for germination:
      40°F–75°F (4.5°C–24°C)
Sun: Full
Water: Water often
Days to germinate: 5 to 10
Days to maturity: 60 to 150
Preferred soil pH: 6.0–7.0

Savoy cabbage

About Cabbage

Cabbage is a nutrient-rich member of the brassica family that is used culinarily across many cultures. It can be eaten raw, pickled, fermented, and cooked. In addition to being high in vitamins K, C, and B6, cabbage contains dietary fiber and a broad spectrum of minerals, including magnesium and iron. It is available in savoy (crinkled leaf), green (smooth), red, and Napa types.

Growing Cabbage

Cabbage is a heavy feeder and requires full sun to form a head. Like most other brassicas, it grows best in cool-season temperatures. Amend soil with plenty of organic matter prior to planting and top-dress with compost and fertilizer throughout the growing season to ensure continued production. Cabbage can be challenging to grow because of its need for additional nutrients, consistent moisture, and susceptibility to pests. Start seeds indoors six to eight weeks prior to last frost, or in late summer for early fall planting in warm-winter climates. Keep soil covered with mulch to help retain moisture.

Harvesting Cabbage

As cabbage grows, the center leaves form a head that becomes firm over time. Check firmness as the head fills out; it will be ready to harvest when the head is full and the leaves resist squeezing. Cut the head just above soil level. Some gardeners leave the stem in the ground to produce three or four baby cabbages after the main head is harvested. This takes time, however, so pull the plant if you need the space for a new crop.

Common Problems

See Broccoli for information on cabbage worms and aphids. Cabbage is more prone to aphid infestations because it's filled with nooks and crannies—safe havens for aphids to hide. Slugs and sowbugs also find cabbage appealing. Cutworms can mow down young seedlings, so plant new seedlings inside a cardboard collar to prevent injury. In northern climates, root maggots can be an issue.

Carrot

Latin name: *Daucus carota* var. *sativus*
Planting depth: ⅛"–⅜" (0.25–1cm)
Plant spacing: 3" (7.5cm)
Soil temperature for germination:
    50°F–80°F (10°C–26.5°C)
Sun: Full to partial
Water: Moderate
Days to germinate: 6 to 18
Days to maturity: 65 to 75
Preferred soil pH: 5.5–7.5

Pusa Asita, Cosmic Purple, Yellowstone, and Danvers Half Long carrots

About Carrot

Carrots are an excellent source of beta carotene, which your body converts into vitamin A, a crucial nutrient in maintaining great eyesight. They can be eaten raw or cooked and are available in color varieties ranging from yellow or white to orange or purple.

Growing Carrot

Carrots can be grown 16 per square foot (0.1 sq m), or hexagonally planted on 3" (7.5cm) centers. Seeds can take between 14 and 21 days to sprout, so watch over them carefully and don't forget to water daily. Carrots prefer cool temperatures, so plant in early spring or late fall. Temperatures higher than 75°F (24°C) can cause low-quality carrots. Once roots have developed, water the plants as required to keep the soil moist to about 3" (7.5cm) deep. Plant in well-amended soil and fertilize as plants grow to ensure proper development (monthly for sandy soil, less often for clay).

Harvesting Carrot

Depending on the variety, carrots should be ready for harvest approximately 55 to 75 days after planting. Check the diameter by running a finger around the shoulders of each root to determine size. This will also loosen the soil, making it easier to harvest. When the top of each root is about 1" (2.5cm) in diameter, it's ready to pick. To prolong the shelf life of carrots, break off the green tops and compost or juice them—or feed them to your worms or chickens for a tasty treat.

Cauliflower

Cauliflower

Latin name: *Brassica oleracea* var. *botrytis*
Planting depth: ¼"–½" (0.5–1.25cm)
Plant spacing:
1 per square foot (0.1 sq m), or
15"–18" (38–46cm) apart if desired
Soil temperature for germination:
55°F–85°F (13°C–29.5°C)
Sun: Full
Water: Moderate
Days to germinate: 3 to 10
Days to maturity: 70 to 80
Preferred soil pH: 5.5–7.5

About Cauliflower

Cauliflower is a cool-season vegetable that is considered a delicacy in both India and Malaysia. It is a more advanced crop to grow; gardeners in higher-altitude areas tend to have better luck, but don't let that deter you from trying. In warm-winter climates, cauliflower grows best in fall, but no matter where you live, this veggie requires nutrient-rich soil and a decent chill to form a head. Coastal gardens may not get enough chill hours to trigger head formation, just giant leaves. If that's the case, try growing Romanesco instead. It has a broccoli growth habit with cauliflower flavor.

Growing Cauliflower

Start cauliflower seeds indoors first and then transplant to your garden after six to eight weeks. (One plant per square foot [0.1 sq m]—they get big!) Transplant them to the garden about 10 days after last frost. Water them well with compost tea to prevent wilting, and water regularly to ensure uninterrupted growth.

Harvesting Cauliflower

Cauliflower is known for its snowy white heads, but it can turn yellow if exposed to direct sunlight. To prevent this, use a clothespin or twine to tie the leaves closed over the heads when the heads are the size of a fist. Check regularly to see if they are ready to harvest. If left too long, cauliflower heads loosen and the tight curds separate, becoming less appetizing. Cauliflower is usually ready to harvest about a week after it's been tied up.

Common Problems

See Broccoli section.

Red celery

Celery

Latin name: *Apium graveolens*
Planting depth: ¼"–½" (0.5–1.25cm)
Plant spacing: 12" (30.5cm) apart
Soil temperature for germination:
60°F–75°F (15.5°C–24°C)
Sun: Full to partial
Water: Water often
Days to germinate: 14 to 21
Days to maturity: 85 to 140
Preferred soil pH: 6.0–7.0

About Celery

Celery can be challenging to grow, but, with the right knowledge, you can easily enjoy homegrown celery. It is a member of the carrot family, and its wild form dates back thousands of years to ancient Greece and Egypt. Celery is fibrous and low in calories, so it is considered a perfect delivery system for fatty, delicious dips.

Growing Celery

Because celery takes upward of three weeks to germinate, it is best started indoors under grow lights. It is grown in late summer or early fall in warm-winter climates, and early spring elsewhere. Transplant into well-amended soil with plenty of compost. Keep soils evenly moist and feed throughout the growing season to ensure large stalks. Celery grows from the center of the plant, and the outer stems tend to lean out.

Harvesting Celery

Individual stalks can be harvested, but the flavor will be much stronger than store-bought varieties. Commercial celery is blanched before harvest, which is easy to do if you plan to harvest the entire plant at once. Tie stalks together at the top and wrap newspaper around the outer edge of the plant, leaving top-growing leaves exposed. Use twine to secure the newspaper. This blocks out the sun, turning the stalks lighter green or white, and reduces the bitterness. Keep wrapped for 10 to 15 days and then cut the whole plant at soil level.

Common Problems

Earwigs and aphids can find a home in tightly packed celery. Use a jet spray to clean off plants occasionally. Put down worm castings at first signs of infestation to ward off sucking insects. Slugs can also appear in moist environments.

Chard, Swiss

Latin name: *Beta vulgaris* subsp. *vulgaris*
Planting depth: ½"–¾" (1.25–2cm)
Plant spacing: 6"–8" (15–20cm) apart
Soil temperature for germination:
    45°F–80°F (7°C–26.5°C)
Sun: Full to partial
Water: Moderate
Days to germinate: 6 to 10
Days to maturity: 55 to 60
Preferred soil pH: 6.0–7.0

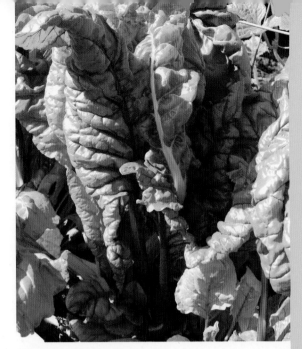

Rainbow Swiss chard

About Swiss Chard

Swiss chard is a member of the beet family but is grown for its leaves rather than its roots. You can find varieties of chard that produce white, yellow, pink, orange, or red stalks. It's great for new gardeners to grow because, in some cases, plants can last for more than a year. It is one of the few vegetables that can be grown in partial sun.

Growing Swiss Chard

Swiss chard can be directly seeded into the garden in early to mid-spring or in fall in warmer climates. The seeds are actually clusters of seeds, so you will get more than one sprout from each seed planted. Thin seedlings to 6"–8" (15–20cm) apart. Keep the seed bed moist to ensure continuous growth.

Harvesting Swiss Chard

Start harvesting the outer leaves when there are several sets of leaves and the plant is at least a 1' (30.5cm) tall. Use a knife or tear stems off at the base of the plant but be careful not to pull too hard—twist instead, and the stems should tear easily from the plant. Hold the plant with one hand if it is still young while harvesting; otherwise, you risk uprooting the whole plant.

Store unwashed leaves in plastic bags with a dry paper towel in the crisper for two to three days. Some gardeners wash the leaves and store them between layers of paper towels in a plastic bag in the fridge. The stalks, which taste like beets, can be stored longer if removed from the leaves. Don't like beets? Cut the stems out and eat just the leaves. See Chapter 10 for a great way to prepare Swiss chard.

Collard greens, bundled for sale

Collard Greens

Latin name: *Brassica oleracea* var. *acephala*
Planting depth: ¼" (0.5cm)
Plant spacing: 12" (30.5cm) apart
Soil temperature for germination: 50°F–75°F (10°C–24°C)
Sun: Full
Water: Moderate
Days to germinate: 3 to 10
Days to maturity: 65 to 80
Preferred soil pH: 6.0–6.8

About Collards

Collards are a cool-season leafy green rich in vitamins and minerals. They tolerate warm weather better than any other member of the cabbage family. Although collard greens are popular in the American South, they can also be grown in northern areas because of their ability to withstand frost.

Growing Collards

Plant seeds in early spring, or in fall in warm-winter climates. If you choose to scatter seeds and then thin, don't toss those thinnings. Throw them into a salad or sauté them instead. Keep the soil moist during hot periods in the summer and control insects and diseases. Collards will reward you with an abundant harvest. Fertilize mid-season to keep plants going strong.

Harvesting Collards

The leaves and stems are edible and can be harvested at any time once the plant is big enough. Pick the larger outer leaves when the plants are 10"–12" (25.5–30.5cm) tall. Like kale and Swiss chard, collards grow from the center, so leave a few sets of leaves to stimulate future growth.

Common Problems

See Broccoli for information on aphids and cabbage worms. Use floating row cover to protect plants from infestation.

Stowell's heirloom sweet corn

Corn

Latin name: *Zea mays*

Planting depth: 1½"–2" (4–5cm)

Plant spacing: 6"–12" (15–30.5cm)

Soil temperature for germination: 60°F–85°F (15.5°C–29.5°C)

Sun: Full

Water: Moderate

Days to germinate: 8 to 14

Days to maturity: 60 to 120

Preferred soil pH: 5.5–7.0

About Corn

Corn is a New World food introduced to early settlers by the First Nation peoples. It is part of the "three sisters" garden (beans, corn, and squash, which grow in concert with one another). Types of corn include sweet, flint, flour, dent (also known as field), and popping. There are hundreds of varieties of corn, although only around a dozen are grown commercially. Corn is a staple food, used to make everything from tortillas to polenta, hominy to posole, masa to muffins, and fresh corn on the cob to popcorn.

Growing Corn

Corn is a heavy feeder, so plant it in well-amended soil. Since corn is wind-pollinated, avoid planting in one long row. Instead, plant in a block of at least three plants by three plants (four by four is better) to ensure proper pollination. Tassels will appear first at the top of each plant, and then silks will appear on each ear. Pollen from the male tassels will fall to pollinate the female silks. Each silk is connected to one kernel of corn inside the husk. Fertilize mid-season as ears develop.

Harvesting Corn

Sweet corn is harvested in the "milk stage," about 18 to 21 days after the silks appear. Silks should be brown. Pierce a kernel with your thumbnail to test for ripeness. If a white liquid is released, the corn is ready to pick. Pull ears down and away from the stalk, and then pull back up to remove from the plant. If the liquid is clear, it's not ready yet. If there is no liquid, the corn is past its prime and can be left to dry on the stalk for flour or cornmeal. For flour and popping corn, let silks turn completely brown; you should not be able to pierce the kernels easily with a thumbnail.

Common Problems

Corn earworms are the larvae of *Helicoverpa zea* moths. The moth lays its eggs on the silks, and the worms eat their way down into the ear, sometimes exiting near the base of the ear. The worms then pupate in the soil. Tricks to prevent this infestation include placing a few drops of vegetable oil on the top of each ear or securing a clothespin around the tip of each ear. Beneficial nematodes applied to the soil help interrupt the worms' life cycle. Beneficial insects such as ladybugs, lacewings, and pirate bugs feed on the eggs and larvae. Additionally, rats and other critters can find corn appetizing.

Protect your corn ears from critters and the rewards will be delicious.

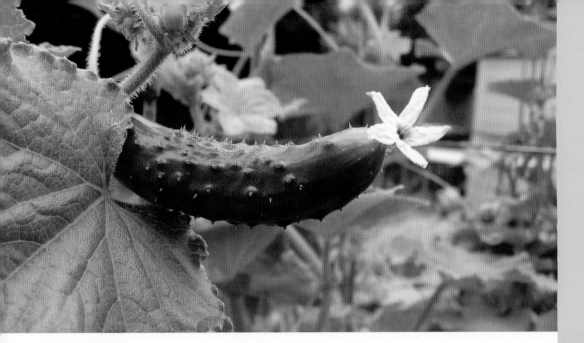
Young cucumbers

Cucumber

Latin name: *Cucumis sativus*
Planting depth: ½"–1" (1.25–2.5cm)
Plant spacing: 6"–12" (15–30.5cm) for vining types; 18"–36" (46–91.5cm) for bush types
Soil temperature for germination: 70°F (21°C)
Sun: Full
Water: Water often
Days to germinate: 3 to 10
Days to maturity: 50 to 70
Preferred soil pH: 5.5–7.5

About Cucumber

Cucumbers are in the same family as squash and melons. The cucumber originated in India more than 3,000 years ago and traveled through Greece, Italy, China, France, and England before arriving in the Americas. While it is technically a fruit, it is commonly referred to as a vegetable. Cucumbers can be eaten raw or pickled; in some cultures, it is cooked into curries.

Growing Cucumber

There are hundreds of varieties of cucumbers that are either vining or bush types. Vining types are best grown on trellises, whereas bush types don't require support. Like other cucurbits, cucumbers don't like to have their roots disturbed, so transplant seedlings carefully or direct-seed in garden soil when soil temperatures warm. Plant in soil enriched with plenty of compost or aged manure. Mulch around each plant to help keep roots cool and reduce infection from soil-borne diseases. Guide vining varieties up their trellises. Fertilize mid-season to ensure continued production. Coastal gardens may not get enough heat to produce an abundant harvest, but they are still worth growing.

Harvesting Cucumber

Snip cucumbers off the vine when they are crisp, firm, and uniform in color. If green varieties begin to turn yellow, they are past their prime. Cucumbers become seedy as they age on the vine, so pick regularly while they are young. Production wanes if fruits are left on the vine too long.

Common Problems

Cucumber beetles and squash bugs attack members of the squash family. Some carry bacterial wilt that causes sudden wilting and death of a plant. Pull infected crops and do not compost them. Apply beneficial fungi and bacteria to the soil to combat infection, and rotate crops seasonally. Powdery mildew is common in coastal climates. Snip off affected leaves. Some products, such as Serenade, which is an OMRI-listed bacterial spray, help prevent infestation if applied at the first signs of trouble.

Grow pickling cucumbers for preserving (making pickles). That way, you can enjoy them in the offseason.

Eggplant

Latin name: *Solanum melongena*

Planting depth: ¼" (0.5cm)

Plant spacing: 12" (30.5cm)

Soil temperature for germination:
    65°F–90°F (18.5°C–32°C)

Sun: Full

Water: Moderate

Days to germinate: 7 to 14

Days to maturity: 70 to 150

Preferred soil pH: 5.5–7.0

Italian eggplant

About Eggplant

Eggplant, also known as aubergine, originated in Asian countries as far back as 300 BCE and migrated to Africa with Persian explorers. This berry (though known widely as a vegetable) comes in an array of colors, including white, purple, orange, and green.

Growing Eggplant

Eggplant is in the same family as tomatoes, peppers, tomatillos, tobacco, and potatoes, so rotate crops to avoid planting this family in the same place for at least three years. It is technically a perennial but is grown as an annual due to its nature as a tropical plant that doesn't overwinter well in snowy climates. In warm-winter climates, second-year eggplant often performs better than first-year. Plant in well-amended soil with plenty of phosphorus to encourage fruit development. Plants may need staking as the season progresses.

Harvesting Eggplant

Pick fruits when they are still shiny and dent slightly under finger pressure. Don't squeeze too hard. Use shears to snip the stems 1" (2.5cm) above the fruit, and wear gloves to protect against spines near the top. Overripe fruits grow dull and turn yellow in color.

Common Problems

Flea beetles eat pinholes in the leaves of eggplants. Sticky traps and diatomaceous earth reduce the beetle population. Larvae pupate in the soil, so apply beneficial nematodes to interrupt their life cycle. Grow insectary plants to attract parasitic wasps and other beneficial insects that prey on flea beetles. Eggplant is also susceptible to powdery mildew and some diseases that affect tomatoes.

Green Onion

Latin name: *Allium fistulosum*

Planting depth: ¼" (0.5cm)

Plant spacing: Ranges from no thinning to 3" (7.5cm)

Soil temperature for germination: 50°F–85°F (10°C–29.5°C)

Sun: Full

Water: Water often

Days to germinate: 4 to 13

Days to maturity: 60 to 65

Preferred soil pH: 6.0–7.0

Green onions

About Green Onions

Green onions, scallions, or bunching onions are a cool-season vegetable that can be grown successfully throughout most of temperate North America (hardiness zones 3–11). In warmer climates, green onions can be grown year-round, and while they are technically perennial, they are generally grown as annuals. According to High Mowing Seed Company, "true bunching onions or scallions, *Allium fistulosum*, do not form bulbs and remain straight and slender; many common onion varieties may be grown as bunching onions, but will eventually bulb up."

Growing Green Onions

Direct-sow seeds in spring or fall by broadcasting (sprinkling seed) or with specific biointensive plant-spacing methods. Seeds can take a while to germinate and grow, and they don't like competition, so keep the area well watered and weeded. As with most vegetables, green onions prefer soils with a lot of organic matter.

Harvesting Green Onions

Pull green onions any time after the green parts are the thickness of a pencil. If left to grow longer, green onions thicken and the taste intensifies. They may be used for cooking when they are too strong to eat raw. Once plants form flower stalks, they are too tough to eat, so let them develop seeds and save those for next year. You can harvest just the green parts and leave the roots intact; the plant will continue to produce more green shoots.

Common Problems

Root maggots can be a problem in higher latitudes. Rust can also settle on green parts of the plants. Cut off affected leaves and thin plants to allow for better air circulation. Rotate crops to prevent rust next year.

Lacinato kale

Kale

Latin name: *Brassica oleracea*
var. *sabellica*
Planting depth: ¼"–½" (0.5–1.25cm)
Plant spacing: 12" (30.5cm)
Soil temperature for germination:
55°F–85°F (13°C–29.5°C)
Sun: Full to partial
Water: Moderate
Days to germinate: 5 to 14
Days to maturity: 50 to 60
Preferred soil pH: 6.0–7.5

About Kale

Kale is the meat of the veggie kingdom—rich in vitamins C and A, and loaded with potassium, calcium, iron, and fiber. Kale can be eaten raw (use an acid like lemon juice or vinegar to make it more digestible) or cooked. Like other brassicas, kale prefers to grow in the cool season and can become sweeter in winter if grown with protection from frost.

Growing Kale

Kale loves full sun but can handle partial exposure if that is all you have. Add plenty of compost or well-rotted manure. Fertilize the plants mid-season with liquid fertilizer or compost tea.

Harvesting Kale

Harvest the outside leaves, leaving the center buds to grow new leaves. Kale will produce all season long. Cut or tear leaves from the base of the plants when they are about 10"–12" (25–30.5cm) long. Kale is delicious in frittatas or cooked in the same way as Swiss chard (see Chard, Swiss).

Common Problems

See Broccoli for information on cabbage worms and aphids. Kale is susceptible to fungal and bacterial diseases like head rot and powdery and downy mildews. Those in coastal areas and other places where these diseases are common should avoid watering from overhead. Check often and remove affected leaves early.

White kohlrabi

Kohlrabi

Latin name: *Brassica oleracea* var. *gongylodes*
Planting depth: ¼"–½" (0.5–1.25cm)
 Plant spacing: 4"–6" (10–15cm)
Soil temperature for germination:
60°F–65°F (15.5°C–18.5°C)
Sun: Full to partial
Water: Moderate
Days to germinate: 5 to 10
Days to maturity: 60 to 65
Preferred soil pH: 6.0–7.5

About Kohlrabi

Kohlrabi is another great brassica that is relatively easy to grow. This European veggie came to America in the 1800s, but despite being around for so long, it is still not a household name. It's an odd-looking vegetable with a bulbous body and leaves that protrude from the top like Sideshow Bob's hair on *The Simpsons*. Don't let that fool you—it has a delicious flavor, similar to broccoli stems and potatoes. Kohlrabi leaves are also edible.

Growing Kohlrabi

Sow seeds indoors in early spring, or in fall in warm-winter climates. If you plan to thin your seedlings, use them in stir-fries or salads. You could plant more every few weeks for a continuous supply through summer. Like other cole crops, kohlrabi tolerates some frost. It also can tolerate partial sun, so plant this crop if you have limited exposure.

Harvesting Kohlrabi

Kohlrabi is best picked when small, but it is not uncommon for gardeners to think bigger is better and let the vegetables grow into the size of softballs. The bulbous part tends to get tough and woody and slightly bitter, so resist the urge to leave kohlrabi in the ground too long. Start harvesting when the stems are about 2" (5cm) in diameter. Peel the tough skin to reveal the inner goodness of this plant. Steam it for eight minutes and then sauté it in a little olive oil or butter until golden for a very potato-like experience.

Common Problems

Cabbage worms are pesky and tend to love kohlrabi, like other brassicas, so keep your eyes peeled and remove them if found.

Leek

Latin name: *Allium ampeloprasum*
    var. *porrum*
Planting depth: ¼" (0.5cm)
Plant spacing: 6" (15cm)
Soil temperature for germination:
    55°F–80°F (13°C–26.5°C)
Sun: Full to partial
Water: Water often
Days to germinate: 5 to 16
Days to maturity: 85 to 90
Preferred soil pH: 6.0–8.0

Leeks

About Leek

Leeks are alliums, part of the onion family. They look like giant green onions, but the green parts are broad and flat rather than round and hollow. Leeks are best known for their pairing with potatoes in soups and stews, and they are a good source of vitamin C. Though they take a while to grow, this is another easy crop—perfect for the brown thumbs out there! Leeks are especially good to grow in cooler climates.

Growing Leek

Leeks like well-amended soil, so prepare garden beds with aged manure or compost and nitrogen-rich fertilizer. Plant seeds in early spring or fall for best results. They will grow in warmer gardening climates, but temperatures over 80°F (26.5°C) will cause them to grow more slowly. Leeks prefer plenty of sunshine. For shorter growing seasons, start with nursery transplants instead of seeds. Mound up the soil around the stems and add more soil to help keep the stems white (this is called blanching). Water them regularly and keep the soil moist but not soggy.

Harvesting Leek

Some gardeners like to cut away a portion of the top leaves in mid-summer. It focuses the plant's energy on growing roots, rather than leaves. Leeks can take up to five months to grow large stems, but they can be harvested as needed when they're smaller. Harvest leeks by pulling, or loosen the soil around the area first and lift them out with a digging fork. Some leeks will cluster together—you will probably end up harvesting those clusters all at once. Leeks store well in the ground, but you should pull them immediately if they start to send up flower stalks. The stalk that runs up the center of the leek is tough and inedible.

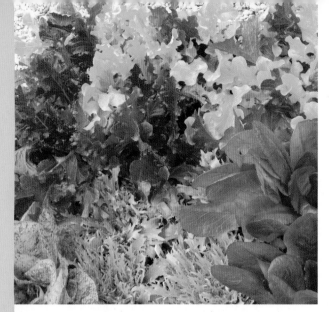
Mixed lettuces

Lettuce

Latin name: *Lactuca sativa*
Planting depth: ¼" (0.5cm)
Plant spacing: 6" (15cm)
Soil: 40°F–80°F (4.5°C–26.5°C)
Sun: Full to partial
Water: Water often
Days to germinate: 2 to 15
Days to maturity: 60 to 70
Preferred soil pH: 6.0–7.0

About Lettuce

Lettuce is a cool-weather vegetable that is easy to grow from seed. There are hundreds of interesting varieties to grow that far surpass iceberg and plain ol' romaine. Lettuces can be planted in early spring or in late summer through fall. In hot weather, lettuce tends to bolt to seed and become bitter tasting. Some varieties handle hot weather better than others, so look for slow-bolt varieties if you plan to grow lettuce in summer.

Growing Lettuce

Plant seeds in well-amended soil and keep the seed bed moist until roots are established. Lettuce has relatively shallow roots, so it can be planted (or interplanted) between crops with deeper root systems. Beware of overwatering, which can lead to diseases and root rot. You can grow lettuce under shade cloth in hot weather to extend the season.

Harvesting Lettuce

Harvest the outside leaves of "cos," or romaine-type, and leaf lettuce whenever they are large enough to use. The plant will continue to produce leaves from the center. Butterhead varieties form loose heads and are generally picked whole by cutting the stem just above the soil level. You can harvest outside leaves for a time and then harvest the entire head when it begins to fill in.

Common Problems

Aphids and pincher bugs (*Forficula auricularia*, commonly known as earwigs) will congregate on the undersides of leaves and in the nooks and crannies of center foliage. Wet weather or overhead watering can result in leaf rot. Check for snails regularly and drop them into soapy water. Place a shallow dish of olive oil to attract earwigs away from plants.

Mustard Greens

Latin name: *Brassica juncea*
Planting depth: ¼"–½" (0.5–1.25cm)
Plant spacing: 6" (15cm)
Soil temperature for germination:
    45°F–85°F (7°C–29.5°C)
Sun: Full to partial
Water: Moderate
Days to germinate: 3 to 10
Days to maturity: 40 to 45
Preferred soil pH: 6.0–7.5

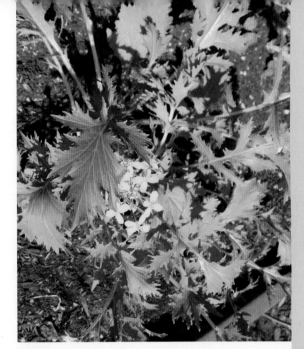

Mizuna mustard greens bolting to seed

About Mustard Greens

Mustard greens are as easy to grow as lettuces from seed. This cool-season cole crop can be grown just about anywhere in the United States during early spring or fall. Mustard greens are high in vitamins A and C and are available in many varieties, including purple-leaf types like Osaka; round, waxy types like Tatsoi; and jagged-edged varieties like Mizuna.

Growing Mustard Greens

Mustard can be planted prior to last frost and all through the cool season. Plant again in mid- to late summer for a fall harvest. Mustard, like arugula, is very quick to sprout, so it's great for growing with kids or those who crave instant gratification. Fertilize mid-season and keep free of weeds. Water regularly to keep the soil from drying out.

Harvesting Mustard Greens

Harvest the outside leaves when they are young—the bigger they get, the spicier these leaves become. Once summer heat comes on, mustard greens typically bolt to seed and become too bitter to eat. If you have chickens, they won't mind the bitter taste, so offload the spent plants onto your hens. Once plants bolt to seed, you can harvest the green seed pods and eat them (they're really spicy!) or save the brown seed pods for next year's seed.

Common Problems

See Broccoli for problems common to all brassicas.

Peas

Latin name: *Pisum sativum* L.
Planting depth: 1" (2.5cm)
Plant spacing: 3"–4" (7.5–10cm)
Soil temperature for germination:
    50°F–80°F (10°C–26.5°C)
Sun: Full
Water: Water often
Days to germinate: 6 to 14
Days to maturity: 60 to 70
Preferred soil pH: 6.0–7.5

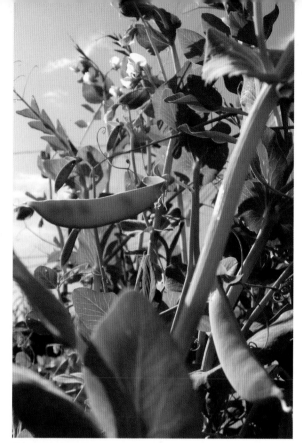

Sugar snap peas

About Peas

Peas are a cool-season vegetable known for being the "garden snack bar," because they rarely make it back into the house uneaten. There are different categories of peas, namely shelling peas, snap peas, and snow peas. Shelling peas require the pod to be removed before eating. Snap peas have been developed over the years to feature less-fibrous, edible pods. Snow peas have flat, edible pods that are usually harvested while the peas are immature. Snow peas are mainly used in Asian dishes. There is another category of pea, called the Southern pea or cowpea (think black-eyed peas), and these are completely different—more like beans, actually—and are grown as a warm-weather crop.

Growing Peas

Peas do best in cool weather and should be planted in early spring or fall. In fact, in warm-winter climates, fall pea crops tend to do better than spring crops. To ensure germination, coat seeds with an inoculant just before planting. Peas should be trellised (though there are some bush varieties that don't require trellises), and, while they have tendrils to grab on to supports, trellises help guide them. Check daily and wind tender vines around trellises. Mulch to keep soil cool and moist; fertilize with compost mid-season.

Harvesting Peas

Harvest peas every couple of days to keep plants producing. Sugar snaps are best when the pods start to fatten, but you should pick them before the seeds fill out. If left too long, peas will become fibrous and starchy. Use these for cooking instead of fresh eating. Harvest by holding the main stem and then breaking or cutting peas from them. Resist the urge to pull, because vines break easily.

Common Problems

Fusarium wilt and root-rot diseases appear as yellowing and wilting of the lower leaves. These diseases work their way up the plant and eventually kill it. Powdery mildew is common in coastal areas, though plants generally produce amply until consumed by powdery mildew. Strive for well-drained soil or choose disease-resistant varieties to prevent Fusarium wilt. Applications of fungal-dominant compost tea can help prevent powdery mildew.

Self-control required: peas are the garden snack that rarely make it back to the kitchen.

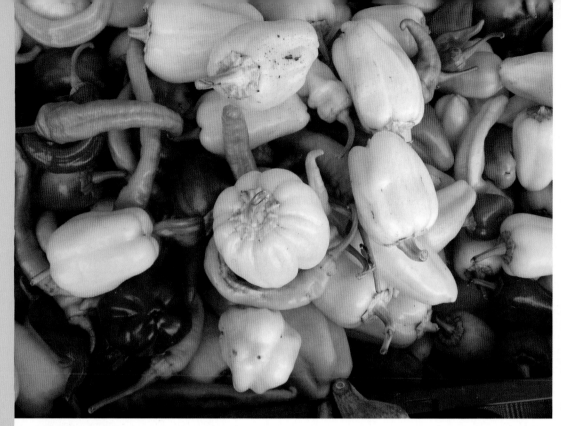

Mixed peppers

Pepper

Latin name: *Capsicum*
Planting depth: ¼"–½" (0.5–1.25cm)
Plant spacing: 12"–18" (30.5–46cm)
Soil temperature for germination: 45°F–85°F (7°C–29.5°C)
Sun: Full to partial
Water: Moderate
Days to germinate: 3 to 10
Days to maturity: 40 to 45
Preferred soil pH: 5.5–7.5

About Pepper

Peppers are hot-weather crops that are technically fruits. They aren't as easy to grow as lettuces and tomatoes, but they are worth having in the garden because of the incredible diversity available. They require high temperatures and tend to grow slowly. Sweet bell pepper varieties are grown for stuffing, and a seemingly endless variety of chili peppers (pimiento, cayenne, chili, and paprika) may be grown for food and spices or as ornamentals. Beginners will benefit by planting nursery stock.

Growing Pepper

Because of their persnickety nature, pepper seeds should be started indoors in late winter and then transplanted out after nighttime temperatures are above 55°F (13°C). Avoid planting them in cold, wet soil. Peppers are heavy feeders, so amend the soil with plenty of organic matter. Water them with compost tea after transplanting. Fertilize after the first flush of peppers set fruit. Keep the plants evenly watered during the harvest season, as inadequate or irregular watering can cause fruit to drop.

Harvesting Pepper

Peppers can be harvested at any size, depending on the variety. Seed packets will help you determine the right time to harvest specific varieties. Some peppers are picked when green, but many continue to turn red, yellow, or orange as they mature. Ripe peppers generally break away easily from the plant, but you must proceed carefully or use shears to cut the stems, so as not to damage the rest of the plant. Chili peppers can be used fresh or dried for later use. Be careful when handling chili peppers because capsaicin, the heat component in peppers, can cause eye irritation and burning. Use gloves and wash your hands well after handling.

Common Problems

Aphids can make their home on weak pepper plants. Maintain healthy soil and nutrient levels, and this will not be a problem. Because peppers are in the Solanaceae family, they can be susceptible to the same diseases as tomatoes and eggplant. Rotate crops yearly to prevent infection.

Grow both sweet and spicy peppers to get the best of both worlds.

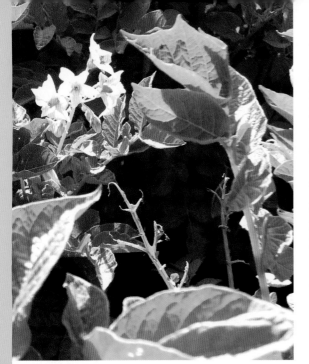

Flowering potato plants

Potato

Latin name: *Solanum tuberosum* L.

Planting depth: 2"–6" (5–15cm)

Plant spacing: 6"–12" (15–30.5cm)

Soil temperature for germination: 60°F–70°F (15.5°C–21°C)

Sun: Full

Water: Moderate

Days to germinate: 15 to 21

Days to maturity: 70 to 135

Preferred soil pH: 4.5–6.0

About Potato

Potatoes are tubers planted in the cool season. Rather than planted from seed, they are grown from seed potatoes or potato cuttings. There are at least 100 varieties of potatoes, ranging from soft or waxy and moist to mealy or firm and dry. There are early, mid-season, and late varieties that work for gardeners in every hardiness zone. You can strategize an extended harvest period (rather than having to harvest all at once) by planting potatoes with both short and long days to maturity. Choose potatoes based on how you like to use them. For example, if you like baked potatoes, choose varieties like Butte, Yukon Gold, or Rose Finn Apple. For sautéed potatoes, try Cranberry Red or All Blue.

Growing Potato

Seed potatoes must be sprouted (made to form eyes) indoors ahead of planting, so plan accordingly. It can take several weeks for sprouts to appear. Sprout potatoes in a shallow box or bucket placed out of direct sunlight, usually under a north-facing window. While you can plant those potatoes that have sprouted in your pantry, best practices recommend purchasing certified disease-free seed potatoes (see Bibliography and Resources for trusted seed companies).

There are different schools of thought about growing potatoes. Some farmers plant shallow (1"–3" [2.5–7.5cm] deep), and then 6" (15cm) of straw or other mulch over the soil. Others plant deeper (about 6" [15cm]) and forgo mulch. Both work. If you live in the North, plant shallow. If you make your home in the South, plant deeper. Either way, more potatoes develop underground if you "hill up" soil or mulch around the plant as it grows. Some gardeners mound soil around the bases; others cover almost all of the foliage with soil, leaving only the top few sets of leaves exposed. The goal is to produce more potatoes and protect surface-dwelling tubers from exposure to sun. Too much sun exposure causes a toxic substance called solanine to develop, which appears as a green hue on the skin. Plant in well-amended soil and use seed potatoes that have developed at least two eyes each. It helps to add organic vegetable fertilizer to the bottom of the trench before planting. Potatoes like foliar feeding with kelp and fish emulsion.

Harvesting Potato

"New potatoes" can be harvested when flowers appear. Pick these without uprooting the plant; gently excavate a few from the sides of the plant while it is still growing. Plant foliage will begin to turn brown and die back when potatoes are nearing harvest. Cut back water at this point. Stop watering about a week before you plan to harvest, and then harvest when all of the foliage is dead. Lift the potatoes with a digging fork or dig with your bare hands to expose the tubers—this is great to do

with kids! Potato skins are soft and scrape easily, so be careful when harvesting with tools. Use damaged potatoes immediately but leave the rest on screens or newspaper out of direct sunlight for a week or so to cure before storing.

Common Problems

Colorado potato beetles, flea beetles, and leafhoppers are the biggest problems with potatoes. Hand-picking pests is recommended. Use floating row cover to protect plants from infestation and practice crop rotation to keep crops disease-free.

Potato math is great: plant one, get a dozen.

Radish

Latin name: *Raphanus raphanistrum*
    subsp. *sativus*
Planting depth: ½" (1.25cm)
Plant spacing: 3"–4" (7.5–10cm)
Soil temperature for germination:
    45°F–80°F (7°C–26.5°C)
Sun: Full
Water: Water often
Days to germinate: 3 to 6
Days to maturity: 21 to 24
Preferred soil pH: 6.0–7.0

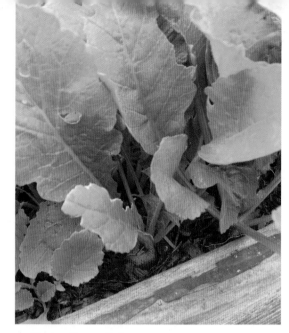

Easter Egg radishes

About Radish

Radishes are some of the easiest vegetables to grow and are perfect for gardeners with short attention spans because they sprout quickly and can be harvested within a month of planting. Radishes are best grown during the cool season, but some varieties are bred for warmer weather.

Growing Radish

Sow seeds directly in the ground where the plants will mature. Radishes tolerate most soils, as long as the soil is fertilized before planting and has adequate moisture. If radishes are not well watered or fed, they can develop slowly, causing them to become woody and spicy. Run a finger through the soil around the diameter of the radish to determine its size before harvesting.

Harvesting Radish

Pick radishes when they are about 1" (2.5cm) in diameter. If grown in the fall, they can stay in the ground longer and be picked as needed once they reach mature size. Both greens and roots are edible and can be used raw in salads or roasted for a delicious treat (see Chapter 10).

Common Problems

In northern latitudes, root maggots can be common. They tunnel into the radishes and leave them in an unsightly state. Garden fabric (floating row cover) will help prevent flies from laying eggs in the soil. Pill and sow bugs (roly-polies) also have been known to nibble away at the tops of radishes. Sprinkle diatomaceous earth to help keep them at bay. Beneficial nematodes can be applied to the soil to help eradicate them as well.

Spinach

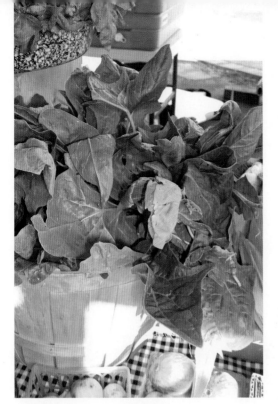

Spinach at a farmers' market

Latin name: *Spinacia oleracea*
Planting depth: ½" (1.25cm)
Plant spacing: 4"–6" (10–15cm)
Soil temperature for germination:
52°F–60°F (11°C–15.5°C)
Sun: Full to partial
Water: Moderate
Days to germinate: 3 to 8
Days to maturity: 40 to 45
Preferred soil pH: 6.0–7.5

About Spinach

Spinach is one of the most highly pesticide-laden commercial crops, so it's definitely one to grow at home. Spinach contains vitamin A, iron, calcium, and protein. Spinach can be grown in spring or fall, during cool weather, and is available in savoy (crinkled) or smooth-leaf varieties.

Growing Spinach

Spinach can be direct-seeded or started in flats in early spring or late summer. Plants prefer well-amended soil that drains well. Use floating row cover if you're direct-seeding, as birds like to hunt for freshly planted spinach seeds. Plant another batch of seeds every two or three weeks for a continuous supply. Fertilize the plants mid-season as needed (if leaves look yellow or small).

Harvesting Spinach

Harvest the outside leaves or cut mature plants at or just below the soil surface. Spinach is of best quality if it's cut while young. Some gardeners prefer to pick the outer leaves when they are 3" (7.5cm) long and allow the younger leaves to develop for later harvest. Once spinach begins to bolt to seed, harvest the entire remaining plant and use it quickly.

Common Problems

Spinach is susceptible to blight caused by cucumber mosaic virus. If your climate is humid or wet, opt for resistant varieties to avoid fungal diseases. Various insects love to munch on spinach. Continue using floating row cover as protection. Regularly check the undersides of leaves for snails and other critters and drop them into soapy water.

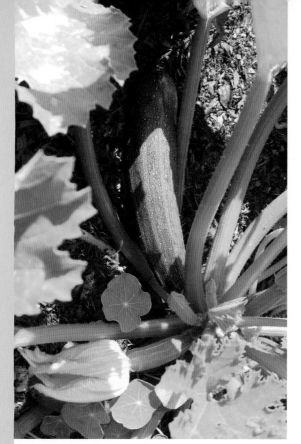

Cocozelle zucchini

Squash, Summer

Latin name: *Cucurbita pepo*
Planting depth: ½"–1" (1.25–2.5cm)
Plant spacing: 3' (0.9m)
Soil temperature for germination:
65°F–90°F (18.5°C–32°C)
Sun: Full
Water: Moderate
Days to germinate: 3 to 8
Days to maturity: 50 to 55
Preferred soil pH: 5.5–6.8

About Summer Squash

Summer squash is a summer staple in the form of zucchini, pattypan squash, and crookneck squash. They are planted as the weather warms up in mid-spring and early summer. You only need one zucchini plant, because it will produce fruit until you're sick of it. Summer squash notoriously grows into baseball bat–sized fruits while gardeners are away on vacation. Harvest regularly to ensure that the plant will keep setting fruit.

Growing Summer Squash

Squash needs space, so allow at least 3' (0.9m) in diameter for each plant. Plant the seeds in a triangle (several seeds in each hole) in the center of the allotted space and thin to the strongest plants as they develop leaves. Amend the soil in the entire area to allow roots to feed in all directions. Mulch around the plants to retain moisture and keep roots cool. Typically, gardeners will plant squash on hills—raised mounds that allow for drainage—but, in sandy soils, the opposite works better; plant seeds in a depression so water collects at the roots when irrigating. You can also create a moat around each plant to deliver water to root systems more easily.

If fruits turn yellow and drop off, it indicates a lack of pollination. Hand-pollinate with a paintbrush by taking pollen from the anthers of the male flowers (which have long stems) and painting it on the stigmas of the female flowers (which have fruit forming beneath them).

Harvesting Summer Squash

Harvest daily once the squash reaches a desired size. Squash can be picked as small as 3" (7.5cm) long, or you can let them grow to club size for stuffing. Generally, summer squash becomes seedy as it grows, so harvest it young for best results. The delicate flowers can be harvested and stuffed, battered, and fried.

Common Problems

As a member of the cucurbit family, squash can be susceptible to cucumber beetles and vine borers. Squash bugs are other common pests that plague winter and summer squash, cucumbers, and melons. Bugs, nymphs, and eggs can be removed by hand and dropped into soapy water. Remove mulch if pests are sighted early on. Tachinid flies are natural predators of squash beetles, so plant umbels around your garden to attract the flies. Organic sprays are available as a last resort to control populations.

Powdery mildew is common in coastal areas. Remove affected leaves or use a mixture of 50 percent water and 50 percent milk to spray on the leaves. Studies show that this helps prevent the spread of the fungus. Fungal-dominant compost tea can also help keep powdery mildew at bay.

You can pick summer squash at any stage, but it is less seedy when young.

Squash, Winter

Latin name: *Cucurbita maxima, C. pepo, C. moschata, C. mixta, C. angeosperma*

Planting depth: 1" (2.5cm)

Plant spacing: 3'–6' (0.9–1.8m)

Soil temperature for germination:
60°F–95°F (15.5°C–35°C)

Sun: Full

Water: Moderate

Days to germinate: 3 to 10

Days to maturity: 80 to 105

Preferred soil pH: 5.5–7.5

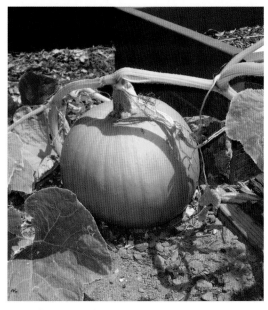

Pumpkin is a winter squash.

About Winter Squash

Remember, winter squash also grows in the summer. The name refers to how long it can be stored. Winter squash has a thick rind, which allows it to last through the winter. There are hundreds of varieties available, from acorn, pumpkin, and Hubbard types to butternut and turban cultivars. Winter squash can be cooked, roasted, or pureed and is commonly used in soups, stews, and pies.

Growing Winter Squash

Like summer squash, winter squash needs room to ramble. Give plants 3'–6' (0.9–1.8m) of space. Early in the growing season, quick crops such as radishes and arugula can be grown in the surrounding soil and then harvested before the squash takes over. Plant the seeds in well-amended soil on mounds or hills (see Summer Squash for sandy-soil alternatives). Plant the seeds in a triangle (a few seeds in each hole) and thin to the strongest plants once they develop several sets of leaves. Like summer squash, winter squash is aided by hand-pollination. Keep it watered to prevent wilting.

Harvesting Winter Squash

Winter squash is easy to harvest; just wait until the foliage dies back and then cut off the stem, leaving at least 1" (2.5cm) of stem attached (squash stores better that way). Some gardeners leave their harvest out in the sun for a few days to cure before storing.

Common Problems

See Summer Squash for pest control and powdery mildew solutions.

Assorted harvested tomatoes

Tomato

Latin name: *Lycopersicon esculentum*
Planting Depth: ¼" (0.5cm)
Plant Spacing: 12"–18" (30.5–46cm)
Soil temperature for germination: 70°F–90°F (21°C–32°C)
Sun: Full
Water: Moderate
Days to germinate: 6 to 10
Days to maturity: 70 to 80
Preferred soil pH: 6.0–7.5

About Tomato

Technically a fruit, tomatoes are the most popular garden crop in America. Curiously, they were considered poisonous until 1820, when Colonel Robert Gibbon Johnson ate a tomato on the courthouse steps in Salem, New Jersey, to prove a point. There is nothing like a homegrown tomato, because most gardeners can grow varieties that wouldn't survive in market conditions. Tomatoes behave as perennials but are grown as annuals in the warm/hot season, because a killing frost will put an end to most tomato plants. They are available as determinate, meaning that they produce all fruit at once, or indeterminate, meaning that they produce fruit over an extended period of time. Coastal gardens may produce smaller tomatoes due to the lack of heat that tomatoes love. Look for varieties originating from mountainous regions; these have been adapted to cooler climates.

Growing Tomato

Start from seed indoors in late winter or buy transplants from reliable sources in spring. Plant out after the threat of frost has passed. Mix in a handful of Epsom salts in the bottom of the planting hole to help prevent blossom-end rot (see Common Problems). Apply compost tea or vegetable fertilizer when transplanting the plants. Fertilize them again after the first tomatoes set fruit and are about 1" (2.5cm) in diameter. Apply fertilizer again after a month or so to keep production going.

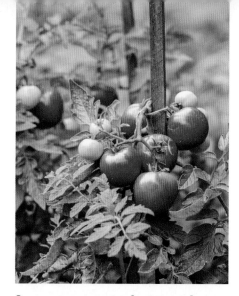

Secure your tomato plants to stakes or use cages to keep them contained in small spaces.

Most people water their tomatoes too much. Once established, water them deeply once per week (in the ground, but more often if in containers). Once they set fruit, water them deeply every 10 days. This encourages roots to dive deep for water. For more detailed information about planting tomatoes, see Homemade Tomato Cages: How to Build a Tomato Crib in Part 2.

Harvesting Tomato

To know when a tomato is ready to pick, cup it between your thumb and two fingers, and rock the tomato back and forth, away from you. A ripe tomato should release from the vine easily. If you have to pull, it's not ready; check back tomorrow. If a killing frost is on its way, harvest all green mature fruit and either wrap each tomato individually in newspaper to ripen over the next several weeks or make fried green tomatoes. Some tomatoes will continue to survive and ripen in winter if plants are laid down and covered with insulated garden fabric.

Common Problems

The tomato hornworm is a fat, green caterpillar with white stripes on its body and a signature horn/tail. Hornworms will eat all parts of a tomato in no time. It's best to handpick them off, though they are well disguised. They can be parasitized by broconid wasps (*Cotesia congregates*), while ladybugs, lacewings, and paper wasps eat hornworm young.

Fungal diseases like Verticillium and Fusarium wilts, early and late blight, and Septoria leaf spot damage leaves and fruit and can even kill a tomato plant entirely. These diseases remain in the soil, so crop rotation is very important.

Blossom-end rot appears as brown, mushy patches on the bottoms of tomatoes. It is caused by both a calcium deficiency and irregular soil moisture. Epsom salts are magnesium sulfate, which assists the plants in calcium uptake.

Crimson Sweet watermelon

Watermelon

Latin name: *Citrullus lanatus*

Planting depth: ½"–1" (1.25–2.5cm)

Plant spacing: 6 seeds per 24"–36" (61–91.5cm)

Soil temperature for germination: 70°F–90°F (21°C–32°C)

Sun: Full

Water: Moderate

Days to germinate: 4 to 12

Days to maturity: 65 to 90

Preferred soil pH: 5.5–6.5

About Watermelon

Watermelons are a warm-weather crop in the Cucurbitaceae family, along with cucumbers, muskmelons, and squash. They were first grown in Africa and then traveled through India, China, and Europe before being brought to the Americas. Watermelons are 90 percent water, containing small amounts of Vitamin C, lycopene, and carotenoids.

Growing Watermelon

This vining crop sprawls toward the sunny side of the garden if left unchecked. Sow seeds or plants near the south edge of raised beds to keep plants from taking over the entire bed. The plants do not root along the vines, so vines can be moved out of pathways and coiled around the main roots. Watermelons prefer moist but not soggy soil. Amend soil with plenty of compost and worm castings to support the watermelon's needs as a heavy feeder. Coastal gardens may produce smaller watermelons due to the lack of heat in summer. Try icebox varieties instead.

Tendrils and both male and female flowers form along the vine. Male flowers appear prior to female flowers. Once fruit is set, you can prune the vine back to two leaf nodes after the fruit. This will focus the plant's energy on increasing the size of the fruit. Avoid overpruning, which can reduce overall production.

Harvesting Watermelon

As watermelons grow, rotate them gently to encourage even coloring. Some gardeners place ripening melons on plates as a barrier for pests. There are plenty of alleged gardening tricks for discerning ripeness, but the best indicator of a ripe watermelon is the vine's tendrils on both sides of the fruit. If they are green, the watermelon is not ready. If the tendrils are brown and shriveling up, it's time to pick.

Common Problems

Like other cucurbits, watermelons are susceptible to powdery mildew in coastal and humid climates. In certain regions, watermelons are also attractive to squash vine borers and cucumber beetles. Spider mites and aphids may attack vines. Worm castings and worm tea offer nutrients and a degree of pest control against sucking insects. See Summer Squash for pest and powdery mildew control.

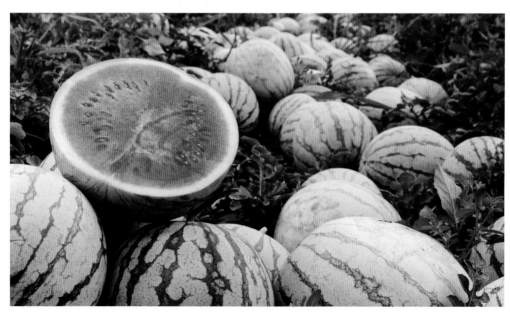

Watermelons are available in varieties with different color flesh, from traditional red to orange and yellow.

HERB PROFILES

Basil

Latin name: *Ocimum basilicum*
Planting depth: ⅛"–¼" (0.25–0.5cm)
Plant spacing: 6" (15cm)
Soil temperature for germination:
    70°F–85°F (21°C–29.5°C)
Sun: Full
Water: Moderate
Days to germinate: 6 to 12
Days to maturity: 65 to 75
Preferred soil pH: 5.5–6.5

Basil, starting to flower

About Basil

Basil is the quintessential summer herb. Its leaves are used in salads, Italian cooking, pesto (see Chapter 10), caprese sandwiches, and more. It is a member of the mint family, but it doesn't take over gardens as mint does. There are many basil varieties available, including Thai, lemon, large leaf, lettuce leaf, and even a few perennial basils, such as African blue or pesto perpetuo.

Growing Basil

Sow the seeds in well-amended, loose soil. Basil can be fussy, so start the plants indoors in spring in cold climates. Water them regularly to keep the seed bed moist and roots cool as the plants develop. Basil will grow more quickly once temperatures warm up. Pinch flowering tips off to keep the plants producing through summer and fall.

Harvesting Basil

Harvest the topmost leaves by picking individual leaves or leaf sets. You'll see two sets of small leaves growing from the nodes along the stem. Pinch the stems with your fingernails or shears just above new growth. Basil can be used fresh, frozen, or dried. Home-dried and frozen basil isn't pretty—it turns black—but it tastes the same in cooked dishes. Freeze basil in ice cube trays in tablespoon-serving amounts or puree it with olive oil and freeze. For best results, dry basil in a dehydrator.

Chives

Chives

Latin name: *Allium schoenoprasum*
Planting depth: ¼" (0.5cm)
Plant spacing: 12" (30.5cm)
Soil temperature for germination:
45°F–95°F (7°C–35°C)
Sun: Full to partial
Water: Moderate
Days to germinate: 7 to 21
Days to maturity: 60 to 70
Preferred soil pH: 6.0–7.0

About Chives

Chives are a perennial herb of Mediterranean origin, related to the onion. They grow in clumps about 10" (25cm) tall and spread in diameter as they mature. Typically used in egg dishes and Asian foods, chives produce a spherical pink flower that is also edible. Another common variety, garlic chives (*Allium tuberosum*), has broad, flat leaves with a seam down the center. Even though they have a different flavor, chives are a great alternative for those with little space to grow full-sized onions.

Growing Chives

Chives can be grown from seed or nursery stock, or by dividing an existing plant. Start the plants indoors or direct-seed in the garden, but note that chives can take up to a year to reach mature size. In warm-winter climates, chives will survive through winter, but they go dormant in cold-winter zones. Water regularly until they are well established, after which chives become somewhat drought tolerant. This herb grows well in partial shade. Fertilize seasonally, as needed.

Harvesting Chives

Cut the chives from the base of the plant, taking small sections each time. Chives will not grow from the cut end but will send up new shoots from the base. Harvesting encourages new growth. Store them in a plastic bag or in a glass of water (like flowers in a vase).

Cilantro

Latin name: *Coriandrum sativum*

Planting depth: ¼"–½" (0.5–1.25cm)

Plant spacing: 4" (10cm)

Soil temperature for germination:
55°F–65°F (13°C–18.5°C)

Sun: Full

Water: Moderate

Days to germinate: 7 to 14

Days to maturity: 45 to 70

Preferred soil pH: 6.5–7.5

Cilantro or young coriander

About Cilantro

Cilantro is a one of those annual herbs that people either love or hate. There are some folks who think it tastes like soap. It's not your fault; it's the aldehydes—fat molecules that also happen to be found in soaps, lotions, and even some bugs. For those who love cilantro, you'll enjoy the fact that it has antibacterial properties that reportedly help fight off salmonella and other food-borne illnesses. Cilantro is one of the easiest herbs to grow (especially in the cool season), and it produces prolific harvests over several months.

Growing Cilantro

Plant cilantro in full sun in early spring or fall, but for best results in hot-summer climates, tuck it behind something taller to give it a little shade. Cilantro bolts to seed quickly, so shade cloth or strategic planting behind taller crops will help prolong the plant's life. According to the University of Massachusetts, Amherst, Center for Agriculture, "The 'seed' of cilantro is actually the whole fruit with two embryos inside. This means that if you plant 10 'seeds' and get 100 percent germination, you will have 20 cilantro plants."

Cilantro can be started indoors or direct-seeded in the garden. When cilantro bolts to seed, the flowers are part of a group of umbels that will attract beneficial insects to your garden. Water regularly, but don't let cilantro get wet feet.

Harvesting Cilantro

Cilantro can be harvested as soon as the plant has about eight sets of leaves. Pick the outside leaves, and the plant will keep producing from the center. If you want coriander for your spice collection, allow several plants to bolt to seed (use only heirloom or open-pollinated varieties if you plan to grow those seeds), and stop watering to let the plant dry out completely. Green seeds form, turn brown, and then can be harvested by cutting off stems and rubbing them between your hands to release the seeds into a paper bag or container. Winnow or sift away the chaff, and store the seeds in an envelope or jar in a cool, dry place. Lazy (or smart) gardeners let cilantro seeds fall in the garden to reseed themselves next season.

Oregano

Latin name: *Origanum vulgare*
Planting depth: ⅛" (0.25cm)
Plant spacing: 12" (30.5cm)
Soil temperature for germination:
    60°F–80°F (15.5°C–26.5°C)
Sun: Full to partial
Water: Moderate
Days to germinate: 5 to 10
Days to maturity: 60 to 80
Preferred soil pH: 6.0–8.0

Oregano

About Oregano

Culinary oregano is a classic perennial herb found in many Mediterranean and Latin American dishes. It can be used fresh or dried, and it blends well with other herbs. The most common variety available at nurseries is called Greek oregano, but a spicy oregano called Mexican oregano (*Lippia graveolens*) is becoming more readily available as well.

Growing Oregano

As a woody herb, oregano is best either propagated from cuttings or purchased as a transplant at a nursery. If you have plenty of patience, feel free to seed it indoors at home, following package directions. Oregano is a spreading herb that trails along the ground, making it a great ground cover for low-traffic areas and ideal for spilling out of containers. Its flowers attract beneficial insects and can be eaten (the flowers, not the insects). Oregano doesn't require heavy nutrients to grow, but it prefers well-drained soil.

Harvesting Oregano

Oregano sends up new growth from the base of the plant, so snip off stems near the soil line as needed once they grow to 4"–5" (10–13cm) long. Oregano tends to get leggy if left alone, and, once it flowers, the whole plant can be cut back to expose new, shorter growth. Some prefer to prune often to prevent oregano from flowering because the plant oils reportedly lose potency once flowers develop.

Common Problems

Spider mites can muddle the appearance of oregano's leaves, and aphids will attack a struggling plant. Use a hose to "wash" the plants regularly and inspect for infestations. Apply worm castings to ward off sucking insects. Organic soap sprays or horticultural oils can be used as a last resort.

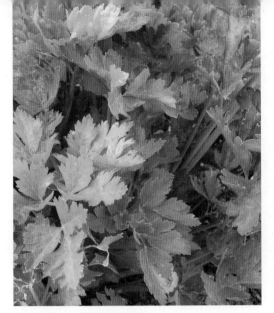

Flat-leaf Italian parsley

Parsley

Latin name: *Petroselinium crispum*
Planting depth: ¼" (0.5cm)
Plant spacing: 5"–12" (13–30.5cm)
Soil temperature for germination:
60°F–80°F (15.5°C–26.5°C)
Sun: Full to partial
Water: Moderate
Days to germinate: 14 to 21
Days to maturity: 75 to 85
Preferred soil pH: 5.0–7.0

About Parsley

Parsley is a leafy biennial herb that is used to flavor and decorate dishes of all cultures. There are several varieties commonly available, curly and Italian flat leaf being the most popular. Parsley is grown as an annual in warm climates because it tends to bolt to seed after one hot season. In cooler climates, you may be able to coax another year out of the plants. Parsley flowers are umbels, which attract beneficial insects to the garden. Once the plant flowers, however, the leaves are generally too strong to use.

Growing Parsley

Parsley can be started from seed but can take several weeks to germinate. For this reason, many gardeners prefer to use nursery stock. If you do want to start from seed, try soaking the seeds overnight in the refrigerator for better germination. Start seeds indoors in late winter or early spring. Nursery stock can be planted in fall in warm-winter climates. Parsley prefers well-amended soil and mid-season fertilizing as needed.

Harvesting Parsley

Parsley can be harvested as soon as the plant has about eight sets of leaves. Pick the outside leaves, and the plant will keep producing from the center. Leave enough leaves to maintain photosynthesis and generate new growth.

Common Problems

Parsley is often the target for the parsley caterpillar, or what becomes a swallowtail butterfly. If possible, relocate these critters, or leave them alone to let them become adult butterflies. See Oregano for treatment of spider mites and aphids. Occasionally, parsley can be afflicted with a mosaic virus. Pull and destroy affected plants.

Sage

Latin name: *Salvia officinalis*
Planting depth: ⅛" (0.25cm)
Plant spacing:
    12"–18" (30.5–46cm)
Soil temperature
    for germination:
    60°F–70°F (15.5°C–21°C)
Sun: Full
Water: Moderate to low
Days to germinate: 10 to 21
Days to maturity: 14 to 21
Preferred soil pH: 5.5–6.5

Purple sage

About Sage

Culinary sage is just one of many varieties of sage available in the plant world. It belongs to the genus *Salvia*, which extends to nonedible and drought-tolerant plants that grow well in Mediterranean climates. It is a woody perennial with leaves that add earthy balance and flavor to winter squash dishes. Gardeners can grow gray, purple, or variegated sages to add color to the garden.

Growing Sage

While sage can be grown from seed, it is best propagated from cuttings or plant division. It prefers a sunny location with well-drained or even sandy soil. It is a drought-tolerant plant, but, once established, it enjoys a deep watering every couple of months, and it benefits from an occasional foliar feeding of compost tea. Plant nursery stock in spring, or in fall in warm-winter climates, where sage overwinters well. It grows well in containers, but small pots may need additional watering.

Harvesting Sage

Sage can be harvested leaf by leaf as needed. Cut just above a leaf node if you're using a whole stem. It's a good idea to leave several stems to ensure that new growth will continue. Use sage fresh or dry it by hanging it upside down or laying it on paper towels. It can be crumbled or "rubbed" and stored in glass jars for later use.

Thyme

Thyme

Latin name: *Thymus vulgaris*

Planting depth: ¹⁄₁₆"–⅛" (0.1–0.3cm)

Plant spacing: 6"–12" (15–30.5cm)

Soil temperature for germination: 60°F–70°F (15.5°C–21°C)

Sun: Full to partial

Water: Moderate

Days to germinate: 21 to 28

Days to maturity: 180 to 240

Preferred soil pH: 5.5–7.0

About Thyme

Thyme is another classic perennial, woody herb used in Mediterranean cooking. Nurseries carry an assortment of varieties, including lemon, English, French, variegated, and common thyme as well as creeping and woolly thyme (for ground cover). Thyme oil is used medicinally and in teas to resolve a number of ailments.

Growing Thyme

Like other woody herbs, thyme is best propagated from cuttings or division, mainly because it can take a long time for seeds to germinate and for plants to mature. It prefers full sun but can tolerate some shade. It doesn't require rich soil but needs good drainage, as it doesn't like wet feet.

Harvesting Thyme

Once established, thyme can be harvested as needed. The plant grows from the cut end, so to ensure a compact plant, give thyme a haircut several times per year by cutting back at least one-third to half of the growth. Blossoms attract beneficial insects to the garden and can be tossed into salads (again, the blossoms, not the insects).

Common Problems

See Oregano for treatment of spider mites and aphids. Ants find thyme to be a favorite place to build nests. In wet conditions, roots can rot and plants can develop mold. Keep well drained and check regularly for ants. Borax-based ant traps are the closest thing to organic controls for ants; use in situations of extreme infestation.

Mark your herbs with plant tags to make them easy to identify.

10 BEST CROPS FOR KIDS

Kids have short attention spans and sensitive palates (they haven't burned off their taste buds with coffee and spicy foods yet). Great veggies to grow with kids fall into three categories: fast * (for impatience), fun Δ (to grow and harvest), and flavorful ▪ (yummy and crunchy). Kids can grow the fast crops on this list for the adults in the family, and the rest for themselves.

	ARUGULA*	A spicy salad green for grownups, which sprouts quickly from seed and grows fast for a speedy harvest.
	CHERRY TOMATO▪	Small fruits you can pop in your mouth for the lunchbox or an after-school snack.
	CILANTRO*	An herb that sprouts in as little as five days with a fun flavor most adults love (and some kids).
	FRENCH BREAKFAST RADISH*	A radish variety that is pinkish-red and white that is best eaten with butter. Kids may not like the flavor, but they love growing this quick-to-maturity veggie.
	LITTLE FINGERS CARROT Δ	Small carrots for small hands. These short carrots will grow in shallow planters, containers, or raised beds. A good option for kids' gardens.
	MEXICAN SOUR GHERKIN CUCUMBER Δ	A cucumber that looks like a tiny watermelon? These cucumbers grow on a vining trellis, and while they take longer to grow, the result is worth it. Don't let the word "sour" put you off—they taste like cucumbers with lime overtones.
	POTATO Δ	Potatoes of all colors are easy to grow at home. Dig for buried treasure when it comes time to harvest. It's a great excuse to get dirty.
	PUMPKIN Δ	Pumpkins are fun to grow every summer, and if you plan ahead, you can grow your own carving pumpkin for Halloween. Enjoy the toasted seeds as a snack, too!
	ROMAINE LETTUCE▪	Crispy lettuces are more appealing to kids, and Romaine fits the bill. Harvest the outer leaves to keep the plant growing for three months or more.
	SUGAR SNAP PEA▪	Peas are the garden snack. Eat them straight from the vine, including the pods. They are sweet when eaten raw and full of nutrients.

10 BEST CROPS FOR BALCONIES OR PATIOS

Container gardening affords gardeners without land the opportunity to grow food close to home. These crops are suitable for growing in pots, small trough planters, and vertical gardens because they take up less space, have a short root system, or can grow vertically. Most of these crops are factory vegetables that keep producing from the same plant, which conserves space and makes your container garden more productive. Choose large pots (at least 12"–15" [30.5–38cm] diameter) for more successful results.

	ARUGULA	Arugula (like lettuces and mustard greens) grows well 6" (15cm) apart, or four per square foot. You can fit four plants in one 12" (30.5cm) pot and have more arugula than you'll ever need.
	BASIL	Most basil varieties grow well in containers and love full sun. Try growing purple, green, and variegated varieties together in a large pot, or separately in smaller pots.
	KALE	Kale is a factory vegetable that keeps giving throughout the season. Try lacinato, red Russian, and curly varieties for a colorful and tasty display.
	LETTUCE	Lettuces grow in small spaces and produce over several months. Plant a mix of romaine, bibb, and oak leaf types in one long trough planter for salad greens all season long. See Arugula for spacing.
	MUSTARD GREENS	Mustard greens add color and texture to any container garden. Try giant purple, tatsoi, and mizuna together. See Arugula for spacing.
	PARSLEY	Flat and curly parsley do well in less sunny spots. Keep a pot close to the kitchen door to add sprigs to your meals.
	PEAS (FULL SUN)	Peas grow vertically on a trellis, taking up less space on a deck or balcony. Eat them while tending to your other plants, or freeze shelled peas for later.
	PEPPER (FULL SUN)	Peppers come in all shapes, colors, and flavor profiles. Choose sweet bells or spicy chilis to add depth and color to your container garden.
	STRAWBERRY	Strawberries do well in half-whiskey barrels or vertical planters with plenty of sunlight. Plant both everbearing and June-bearing varieties to extend your growing season.
	SWISS CHARD	Swiss chard has beautiful stems that come in gold, yellow, white, pink, red, and green. The leaves have a spinach flavor, and the stems taste like beets. So it's like getting two veggies in one.

10 BEST CROPS FOR SENIORS

To make the best use of time, energy, and money, perennial crops are the way to go. They require less effort and care, allowing for more time to do other things. Plant once and enjoy for years to come. And once established, their deep roots don't need as much water and, in some cases, can overwinter without moving them indoors. Most of these crops grow well in containers or elevated planters if deep enough (12" [30.5cm] minimum) to ease mobility issues.

	ARTICHOKE	Artichokes do well in Mediterranean climates and cooler climates if protected. Grow them in pots or in-ground. They die back in late summer or over winter but return year after year. Grow purple and green varieties to keep things interesting.
	ASPARAGUS	Asparagus is a commitment—it takes three years to establish plants, but then you can harvest from these plants for 20 years. Don't wait to give this pricey veggie some space in your garden.
	BLUEBERRY	Berries of all kinds are great to grow for a yearly harvest. Give them acidic soil, prune them at the end of the season, and they will return the favor in abundance.
	CHIVE	Perennial herbs like chives expand over time and can be divided as they grow. Give away plants to friends or expand your herb collection.
	OREGANO	Oregano is eaten fresh or dried. It requires little attention other than a seasonal haircut. This no-nonsense herb pairs well with taller perennials.
	RHUBARB	Rhubarb emerges early from the garden and works in both sweet and savory dishes. Give it space to grow, and it will reward you with an early harvest each year.
	SHALLOT	Alliums including shallots take a full season to grow and need little attention along the way. They store well once harvested. Grow your year's supply in as little as 4 sq ft (0.4 sq m).
	SWEET POTATO	Sweet potatoes come back year after year in warm-winter climates. Gardeners with mobility issues can grow these in pots and tip over to harvest.
	SWISS CHARD	Chard can live longer than a year and is one of the more productive factory vegetables. They are even beautiful when they bolt to seed, so there's no hurry to clean them up at the end of the season.
	THYME	Thyme (like oregano) works well in small spaces, and only needs a haircut once or twice per season. Use sprigs in cooking, or dry them for winter use.

CHAPTER 7

Irrigation

I t's simple: If vegetable crops and young fruit trees don't have water, they die. Conversely, most plants will thrive if you simply water them. Sure, fertilization, sun exposure, and pest management are all part of tending a garden, but without water, there is no vegetable garden to tend. With climate change and desertification happening all over the world, water has become scarce in places that need it most.

For example, in recent years, central California farms have been severely affected by drought. Many farmers left acres of land uncultivated because water rations were too tight. The farming industry is moving toward more efficient irrigation methods, but you can still drive along California's Interstate 5 at noon on 100°F (38°C) days, and you will see overhead sprinklers in action.

A long water trough supports herbs and vegetables through the growing season in this aquaponic garden.

We home gardeners are fortunate. We don't have to shell out thousands of dollars for miles of drip tubing. With very little effort, we can easily design and install efficient irrigation systems for our little patches of land. There are many ways to approach this task, depending on the philosophy to which you subscribe. There are ancient techniques to sequester water in soils, rainwater catchment systems, in-ground PVC sprinklers, above-ground drip systems, gray-water systems, and good old-fashioned hand-watering. Let's explore different approaches to giving your garden the moisture it needs.

Hand-Watering

If you want to live the simple life, with low-tech solutions for watering your garden, nothing beats a watering can or a garden hose with a good-quality spray nozzle. Watering tools are widely available from bargain-basement to high-end models, so it's good to know what to look for when you're shopping.

Watering Cans

A good watering can has two handles: one on top and one opposite the spout, making it easier to carry and pour. A good can also holds enough water so you don't have to run back to your water source frequently. A 2 gallon (7.5L) watering can is light enough to carry when full but will hold a sufficient amount of water for the job.

The spout on a watering can should have a good rose on the end. The smaller the holes in the rose, the finer the delivery of water. The goal is to mimic rainfall, allowing soils to absorb moisture at a slow rate rather than the water pooling on the surface, so pinholes are best. The rose should be removable, allowing you to clear out leaves and other gunk that collect at the bottom of the can.

While those galvanized metal watering cans are beautiful, avoid them. Not only are they heavy and cumbersome, but they are coated with zinc, which can leach into the water and remain in the soil, locking up nutrients from plants. Haws, a British company who has been making watering cans since 1886, makes a terrific product that fulfills all of these criteria: their 1.6 gallon (6L) Practican is the envy of many a gardener.

A good-old garden hose can get the watering job done.

Garden Hoses

Garden hoses have become more complicated as plastics have evolved. We were once limited to standard green garden hoses that kinked and split, but now there are a plethora of options for home gardeners, including coil hoses and kink-free, drinking-water-safe hoses, with color choices in every hue of the rainbow. There are even coil hoses that come with adapters to connect to your kitchen sink, in case you don't have access to a hose spigot outside.

Back up a second. Drinking-water-safe? "Aren't all hoses drinking-water-safe?" you ask as you think back to your childhood memories of slurping from the sprinkler nozzle on a hot summer day. Definitely not. Most hoses are made from polyvinyl chloride. As it happens, lead is used as a stabilizer when working with polyvinyl chloride, and there it remains until you use the hose to water your plants.

According to Ecology Center, which did a study on drinking-water-safe and regular hoses in 2016, between 5 and 500 times the allowable levels of lead were found in samples from hoses not labeled as drinking-water-safe. The report recommends flushing the water from the hose before using it each time. The same study found high levels of bromine, tin, and phthalates in garden hoses, some of which leached into the water. It isn't just hoses—these chemicals can be found in garden gloves, kneeling pads, and tools. It pays to do your research. Look for labeling to ensure that what you buy is drinking-water-safe.

A word about coil hoses. They can be great because you don't have to wind them up at the end of the day, but they can be annoying because once they tangle, it's challenging to restore order to the mess. Here's a hint: opt for coil hoses that are ⅝" (1.6cm) in diameter rather than ½" (1.25cm). The thicker diameter prevents the hose from twisting into itself as much. Newer coil hoses are even thinner—⅜" (1cm) in diameter. Use these at your own risk, as they tend to tangle up easily.

Hose Nozzles

Watering your garden is much easier if you have a spray nozzle attached to the end of your hose. While one can certainly admire the art of thumb-over-the-hose-end techniques, your seedlings will appreciate the gentle, even spray that a nozzle can provide. Your housemates will also thank you for a lower water bill. A sprayer nozzle keeps water from flowing from the hose until you need it, and many nozzles offer different settings for all your gardening tasks. Use the "mist" setting on newly planted

While orach mountain spinach grows well in the hot summer, it still needs water.

seeds or seedlings, "shower" for everyday watering that mimics rainfall, and "jet" for blasting bugs and cobwebs from infested trees and plants.

As product manufacturing migrated to other countries, the quality (and price!) of spray nozzles noticeably decreased, but there are still good-quality sprayers available. The key is to find one made from metal, not plastic. Plastic sprayers break down in less than a year, but metal sprayers hold up much longer. The only exception to this is a fan sprayer. Those classic yellow Y-shaped sprayers are the cheapest things around, and, for some reason, they work better than some expensive nozzles. The crew at Ecology Action uses fan sprayers because they mimic rainfall very well and are inexpensive, an important feature for thrifty gardeners who follow GROW BIOINTENSIVE methods. You can prolong a sprayer's life by soaking the head in vinegar to remove hard-water deposits, so try that before buying a new one. For a little more excitement, add baking soda and watch the bubbling action eat away at deposits.

If you plan to water by hand, keep in mind that there are optimal times to do it. Mornings before 9:00 and afternoons after 4:00 are best. In sunnier, hotter parts of the day, water will evaporate before your plants have a chance to absorb it. There are differing schools of thought about when to water. Some experts emphatically recommend watering only in the morning, because evening watering can lead to mildew or rot. Experts on the other side of the fence firmly believe that we should water only in late afternoon, so plants can use the moisture overnight to grow. It really depends on your climate. If you live in an area that is humid or shrouded by marine layer, watering in the morning might be best to allow plant leaves to dry out before the clouds roll in later in the day. For those with hot, dry days, watering at night will ensure a longer period of access to moisture without the threat of evaporation. The bottom line is to see what works for you.

Some gardeners prefer to drizzle water at the soil level with a bucket and cup, or they fill up water bottles and connect them to special cones that sit below ground to deliver water at root level. The Native Americans were introduced to Spanish ollas, which came to Spain from Africa, as a method for watering underground. Ollas are unglazed jugs with long necks that are buried in the ground, leaving only the jugs' open mouths exposed. Gardeners fill these jugs with water, which seeps through porous walls into the soil right where the roots need it. Water seeps to about 9" (23cm) out from the jugs, so plants don't need to be right next to them. Ollas are still used today in gardens to conserve water.

Drip Irrigation

Some claim that science-minded gardeners are obsessed with drip irrigation. It's all about coming up with the coolest, most clever system that is completely invisible and uses the least amount of water with no overspray. Just a quick walk down the garden plumbing aisle at the hardware store will give you a sense of just how many possibilities there are for above-ground irrigation: ½" (1.25cm) tubing,

Quarter-inch (0.5cm) tubing with 6" (15cm) emitters works better and is more flexible in small-space gardens than ½" (1.25cm) tubing with 12" (30.5cm) emitters.

¼" (0.5cm) tubing, tubing with or without emitters, and soaker hoses that sweat. Then there's the array of emitters to choose from: spider bubblers, flag emitters, inline flow emitters, pressure-compensating emitters, microsprayers, microsprinklers, microsprayers with flow-control valves, and even fogger/mister attachments. Oh, the possibilities!

Think of drip irrigation like the ultimate LEGO® set. All of the pieces fit together in a hundred different combinations. Some pieces are specialized, but there is logic to how they fit together. You have tubing attached to connectors, which connect to more tubing. Good-quality connectors are usually barbed so that they hold in place better, and they can be straight (inline), elbows, or tees. There are also plugs, called end caps, to close off the tubes, and even plugs called goof plugs (no lie) for patching up holes you didn't mean to make.

To connect the tubing to a water source, there are a few other parts to consider. First, a timer is connected to the hose spigot to control the frequency and duration of water flow. Next is a series of backflow preventers, filters, and pressure regulators that screw together and eventually end with a connection to the drip tubing that will inevitably reach your garden. Not all of these parts are necessary in every situation; it

Quarter-inch (0.5cm) drip tubing with a tee connector is used for irrigating a vertical garden system.

Low-cost, above-ground irrigation is easy to install with battery operated timers that connect directly to a hose bib.

depends on your water source, the size of your system, and how much you are willing to invest.

For a small and simple system, a gardener might disregard the need for a filter or a pressure regulator. If you have control over your hose spigot, and leave it turned on in the same place all the time, chances are you won't have enough variance in water pressure to burst the tubing. And given that most timers come with a screen filter on both ends, they eliminate the need for a flushable filter in many cases. However, if you are attaching drip irrigation to an underground sprinkler system, don't skimp on the pressure regulator or filter. The extra expense is worth not having to dig the whole thing up later.

Water: How Much/How Often?

When it comes to irrigation, soil behaves like a sponge. Have you ever tried to wipe up a spill with a dry sponge? Rather than absorbing the spill, it just pushes it around. Soil does the same thing when it's very dry. You may have to slowly wet the soil for a few days before it can absorb water, just as you have to wet a sponge thoroughly and squeeze it out before it can sop up a mess. Keeping soil moisture consistent will help you water less each time you irrigate, because the water will penetrate properly. A layer of mulch will help retain moisture.

If you see your squash plants wilting after the day's heat has subsided, your plant needs more water.

For hand-watering, start with a gentle setting on your sprayer nozzle and be patient. If water starts to pool up, turn the hose down or pause for a minute. Watch for what John Jeavons calls "the shiny." It's that moment when water soaks into the soil and glistens on the surface for about one or two seconds as it sinks down. Once you achieve "the shiny," repeat the process until the area is thoroughly irrigated.

When using drip irrigation, it's a good idea to know just how much water is being delivered to your garden. Some cities have laws requiring drip systems to operate efficiently, below a maximum "inches per hour" flow rate. Russell Ackerman, the water resource specialist for the City of Santa Monica, California, is an expert in drip-irrigation math, and his formula for calculating drip-system precipitation rates is too scientific to resist. Put on your math caps as you read through his calculations on page 215.

Even with nifty rule-of-thumb formulas, though, irrigation is not an exact science. A lot depends on your soil structure and the types of plants you are growing. That's why most watering instructions for vegetables are vague, such as "requires moderate water" or "let soil dry out between waterings." Remember, clay soil will hold water longer than sandy soil. Seeds and seedlings will probably need water every day until root systems develop. Once plants grow in and form a living mulch over the soil (or you add a mulch layer), less water is needed. In the end, your soil and plants will tell you if they are getting enough water. You can use the "two-knuckle test" (see the sidebar on the opposite page) to monitor your soil's moisture level.

Plants have their way of sending signals about moisture, too. Plants wilt or change color when something is wrong. If a plant turns brown and crisp, that usually means it didn't get enough water. If it turns yellow, that usually means its roots are suffocating from too much water—not enough oxygen in the soil. Yellow can also mean that your plants need nitrogen, so if cutting back on water doesn't solve the problem, perform a soil test to determine nutrient deficiencies.

If you see your plants wilting during the warmest, sunniest part of the day, resist the urge to throw water on them immediately, unless they are new transplants. Instead, wait until late afternoon and inspect the plants again. If they are still wilted after direct sunlight has passed, they need water. Some plants, like tomatoes, have a defense mechanism to curl up during the hot part of the day. They perk back up after sunset like nothing was ever wrong. Don't be fooled.

Given that your situation is going to be unique, and you will learn about your garden's irrigation needs through trial and error, here is a less-vague suggestion for watering a typical raised-bed vegetable garden: set your drip timer for three days per week for ten to fifteen minutes. You can hand-water newly planted seeds and seedlings on the off days to ensure the seed beds stay consistently moist. Reduce the days per week during the rainy season as needed and shut irrigation off completely on rainy days. Many timers are equipped with a rain-delay setting.

Water Catchment: Rain Barrels, Gray Water, and Other Ways to Capture Water

If we're striving to be as sustainable as possible in our gardens, it makes sense to create ways to sequester water in the soil or utilize rainfall, rather than to pump water in from municipal sources. Because yearly rainfall varies from hardiness zone to hardiness zone, your need to capture water may be more important than it is for others. For example, upstate New York averages 40"–50" (102–127cm) of rain per year. Los Angeles gets only 12"–15" (30.5–38cm)—and it all happens over three or four months. So what's a person to do when it's not raining? Let's look at the options for water catchment.

Rain Barrels

These containers are placed under the downspouts of rain gutters to funnel rainfall from the roof. The amount of water that can be collected this way is staggering if you have room for enough rain barrels or a cistern. Here's the formula, using imperial measurements:

$$\text{(area of roof in square feet) x (inches of rain per period) x (0.6 gallons per inch of rain per square foot) x (0.75) = (gallons/period)}$$

First, calculate your surface area by multiplying the length and width of your roof in feet (including the gutters).

Next, choose a number of inches of rain per period that you want to capture and store. For simplicity, let's assume the period we're interested in is one day. The average daily rainfall in your hardiness zone can be found on just about any weather website. For simplicity, let's choose 1" of rainfall per day.

The next number (0.6) represents the standard number of gallons of water that can be collected for every inch of rain, for every 1,000 sq ft of roof. (**Note:** If using metric measurements, this is 2.3L of water per 2.5cm for every 93 sq m of roof.)

The number 0.75 is a rule-of-thumb efficiency coefficient for collecting roof water. Think of this as the margin of error, or nature's way of keeping some of the harvest. This number will vary from climate to climate, and from roof to roof, but 0.75 is a good starting point.

Now you have the number of gallons per day you can collect from your roof with 1" (2.5cm) of rainfall per day. Or, if you prefer, this is the number of gallons (liters) you can collect from your roof with 1" (2.5cm) of rainfall over a period of time.

This is one option for a rain barrel. Some cities sell rain barrels at a subsidized rate to residents.

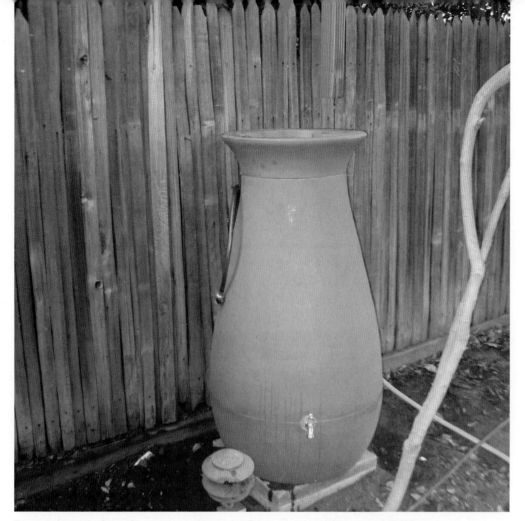

Decorative rain barrels are an option near downspouts with more visibility.

Example: (20' length x 40' width) x (1" rain per day) x (0.6 gallons
per inch of rain per square foot) x (0.75) = (800 square feet)
x (1" rain per day) x (0.6 gallons per inch of rain per square foot)
x (0.75 efficiency) = 360 gallons per day

That's a lot of water from 1" (2.5cm) of rain. Most rain barrels hold 55 or 60 gallons (208 or 227L), so you would need six or seven of them to contain the storm water. (Money-saving tip: your municipal green waste bin holds about 90 gallons [341L], and if you're composting most of your green waste, you can use the bin all winter for water catchment.) There are above-ground cisterns on the market that hold 300–10,000 gallons (1,136–37,854L). Some gardeners have several rain barrels, each under a downspout at a different corner of the house. The downspouts usually need to be cut shorter to spill into the tops of the rain barrels. You can connect overflow hoses to fill up additional barrels if you have room.

If rain is infrequent, you will be able to use up the contents of your rain barrel before the next rainfall. Some gardeners in low-rainfall areas have been able to turn off their irrigation systems completely for six months by using the water collected in just three rain barrels.

Gray-Water Systems

Recycling gray water from household appliances is a touchy subject. For years, it has been illegal in many cities and states, but laws are changing as water shortages populate headlines. A gray-water system can be as simple as placing a bucket in the shower while the water warms up or as complex as having a diverter to redirect washing-machine water to a tank or flower bed. If you plan to use gray water, it's important to remember that you must use biodegradable soaps and detergents.

According to a "white paper" report from the WateReuse Association, the average household generates 39 gallons (148L) of gray water per day from washing clothes and taking showers or baths (gray water typically does not include water from the toilet, dishwasher, or kitchen sink). That's two-thirds of a rain barrel. If you could redirect even part of that wastewater to flower beds or lawns, you could save precious dollars (not to mention gallons) per year.

Check your city ordinances to find out about the laws for gray-water systems in your area. There are DIY books or local professionals who can help—you must have a plan; do not just start redirecting plumbing on your own.

There is much debate over whether gray water can be used to water vegetable gardens. For safety's sake, at this time, gray water is recommended for use only on fruit trees, shrubs, and flower beds.

Swales

Before the invention of drip tape (and even more recently), farm cultures directed water through strategically placed channels to irrigate farmlands. Nature makes its own channels in forests and plains, carving out paths for snowmelt to trickle toward rivers. Along the way, plants benefit from water that is absorbed deep into the soil to be drawn upon later in the dry season. Such is the nature of a swale. Swales (rhymes with "tails") are shallow trenches that not only funnel water along a path but also help

Downhill

Swales

Dig swales into the high side of a slope to sequester water for trees below.

sequester water in underground stores for deep roots to access later. Permaculturists mimic nature by contouring the soil of gardens to direct water where it is most needed. On a hillside where water might ordinarily run downhill, causing erosion, a swale running across the hillside can stop water in its path and trap it underground near crops or fruit trees.

✳ ✳ ✳

Keeping water on site will likely make your garden better. These water-capturing techniques each merit more investigation to learn their subtleties, but, as a good gardener, that shouldn't be much of a problem for you.

CHAPTER 8

Keeping Order: Trellises and Cages for Crops

While science and orderliness often go hand in hand, being a Gardenerd doesn't necessarily mean you are organized by nature. In fact, many gardeners prefer meandering, sprawling garden jungles rather than color-inside-the-lines, pruned-to-perfection gardens. Wherever you fall on the spectrum of order, it's important to remember that vegetables—just like people—grow better if they are well supported.

Pole beans grow up wood and wire trellises.

Choosing the right trellis for a plant can make the difference between success and failure. If you grow peas on a 4' (1.2m) trellis, you will find out the hard way that peas easily grow to a height of 8'–10' (2.5–3m). Without something sturdy to climb, stems can snap or crease as they collapse, shortening the plants' productivity and lifespan. This chapter reviews the various selections of trellising contraptions for tall and vining crops.

Materials for Trellises and Cages

There are as many ways to support a crop as there are crop varieties themselves. Tomato cages alone come in a blinding array of sizes, shapes, and colors. Many gardeners prefer a multipurpose trellis that works for peas, cucumbers, pole beans, melons, and tomatoes. To fit the bill, you may have to build the support structure of your dreams, but there are also commercial options available. Let's look at the practicality of different trellis materials.

Wood

If you want to build an A-frame, permanent trellis in part of your garden, 2x4s should do the trick. While conventional wisdom would say to use pressure-treated lumber, it is not recommended for use around food crops. Instead, paint the bottom portions of the legs with several coats of latex paint and use cedar, redwood, or composite lumber to ensure durability.

Ready-made redwood trellises are available in heights ranging from 3"–10" (0.9–3m) and usually have 7"–8" (18–20cm) grid openings, allowing gardeners to reach through to harvest and tame wild vines. Panels of redwood lattice can be used as trellises, but they lack wide openings for hands to reach through. These panels need a solid framework in order to hold up heavy crops, so avoid panels that are sold without a wooden frame. Lattice is great for attaching to walls or fences.

Willow branches are a natural trellising option for those interested in picking up a new skill set that crosses over from gardening into folk art. The flexibility of willow makes it great for creating curved designs, arches, and even gates or furniture. There are several publications about the art, the most well-known being *Making Bentwood Arbors and Trellises* by Jim Long. Plant a willow tree for a continuous supply of materials in the years to come; you'll also be able to weave your own harvest baskets.

Metal

Half-inch (1.25cm) galvanized pipe is a great starting point for a metal trellis. By creating a frame with two 10' (3m) vertical lengths hammered into the ground, and a crossbar connected by elbow joints, you will have a trellis that will last upward of 10 years. Stretch mesh netting across the frame, or run twine in vertical lines down to the bed, and you'll have a versatile yet permanent trellis that will work for all sorts of climbing crops, including tomatoes.

These lima beans stay upright on a metal trellis that is durable enough to hold the weight.

Chain-link fences make fine supports for vining crops, as do a lot of the folding metal cages and supports that are available commercially. For serious tomato growers, Texas Tomato Cages are the only thing that will do. They're 6' (1.8m) tall, 24" (61cm) in diameter, and made from ¼" (0.5cm) galvanized steel. You won't be using biointensive plant spacing with these cages, but your tomatoes will be well supported.

Coated rebar is indispensable for bracing trellises in the wind or for preventing tall crops from collapsing. Attach 8' (2.4m) rebar stakes on either side of wide, flat trellises for extra support on windy days. When pole beans overtake corn stalks, a common occurrence when growing a "three sisters" garden, rebar stakes come in handy to prop up overbearing vines.

Grow-through supports are dainty, coated metal trellises for short crops or plants that tend to sprawl open as they flower and age. These supports look like miniature tables with three or four legs and lattice tabletops. Install them while plants are young; the shoots will grow through the lattices and stay upright.

Thick-gauge wire and T-posts are used for keeping blackberries and other cane berries in check. Wire can also be used with eye hooks to train grapevines and other climbing vines along a wall or fence.

Bamboo makes a strong, natural trellis material.

Bamboo

This renewable resource is strong and compostable, so if you want to take the natural approach to trellising, bamboo is an excellent choice. Some gardeners grow bamboo on site to have a constant supply. Bamboo can be lashed together to form A-frame trellises or woven together to form lattices. Teepees are typically constructed from bamboo by lashing three or four poles together on one end and securing the other ends in the ground at an angle. Individual stakes can be sturdy enough for supporting determinate tomatoes and some wayward vines. Use stakes that are at least ¾" (2cm) thick. Single stakes of any material are not recommended for indeterminate tomatoes, unless you don't mind having tomato vines all over the place. Use cages instead.

Nylon and Other Plastics

Fishing line is often used to guide espaliered fruit trees or grapevines up a wall. Gardeners install eye hooks in strategic places and weave fishing line to provide places for vines to grab. The line is nearly invisible, and you can add more as needed.

Mesh netting is a great solution for trellising crops that tend to wander such as peas. Cover a sturdy trellis frame with a layer of 7" (18cm) netting and watch vines cover it in no time. Bird netting, which has 1" (2.5cm) mesh, will work for this task, though you can't get your hands through it to harvest crops on both sides.

What Plants to Trellis or Cage

Unwieldy plants come in all shapes and sizes, so there's more than one way to tackle the issue of supporting them. The chart on page 166 will help guide you toward the right kind of trellis for your behemoth blackberry or your arching asparagus. It also includes trailing crops that can be trellised for space efficiency.

Remember, when you use a trellis, most climbing plants will eventually grab on, but they require guidance at first until tendrils have a firm hold.

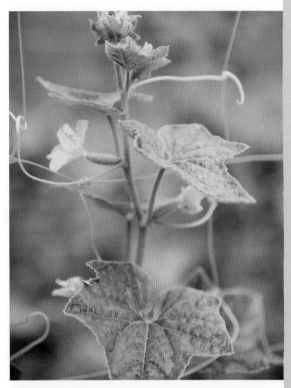

Vinyl mesh netting is durable but won't last as long as metal trellises.

Tomatoes don't have tendrils to grasp supports, so keep a watchful eye on new shoots that will attempt to escape the confines of a cage. Check plants often and gently guide shoots upright. Check out our How to Build a Tomato Crib instructions in Part 2.

Plant Wrangling: Basic Pruning Tips

It happens to everyone, though not all gardeners will admit it. At least once in a while, the garden gets out of control. You go on vacation or turn your back for a few weeks, and suddenly the tomato vines are 3' (0.9m) longer, the melons are trailing over every square inch of pathway, and the cane berries have taken over the back forty. Here are some basic tips for wrestling your vegetable and fruit crops back into compliance.

The Three Ds: Dead, Diseased, and Disorderly

When things get out of hand, it helps to have a starting point—in this case, dead leaves, vines, and branches. Cut those away, and you will begin to see space that allows for a closer look. Diseased plant matter is easy to identify. It's wilted, it's brown or yellow, it has spots, and it basically looks terrible. Cut those away and toss them,

PLANT AND TRELLIS PARTNERSHIPS

PLANT NAME	IDEAL TRELLIS	NOTES
Asparagus	6' (1.8m) stakes in four corners, twine surrounding bed	Tie several levels to catch low and high branches.
Beans, pole	8' (2.4m) sturdy metal frame covered with 7" (18cm) netting	Bamboo teepees with twine around circumference works well. If growing with corn as a trellis, choose very tall corn varieties.
Blackberry/raspberry	4' x 4' (1.2 x 1.2m) posts every 5' (1.5m) with 2' x 4' (61 x 122cm) crossbars	Run 22-gauge wire through tips of crossbars to form outer supports for canes; can use metal T-posts instead of wood.
Cantaloupe (and other muskmelons)	Metal or wooden trellis with 7"–8" (18–20cm) grid spacing	Use old T-shirts or pantyhose to sling fruit to the trellis as it ripens.
Cucumber	8' (2.4m) sturdy metal frame covered with 7" (18cm) netting	Lean-to style wood or metal lattice trellises allow cucumbers to grow while providing shade for lettuce crops beneath.
Fava beans	4'–6' (1.2–1.8m) stakes in four corners, twine surrounding bed	Small groupings may be tied together loosely.
Grains	No trellis needed, but stakes can be used on top-heavy stalks before harvest as with fava beans	
Peas	8' (2.4m) sturdy metal frame covered with 7" (18cm) netting	Bamboo teepees with twine around circumference works well, or a wooden lattice.
Pepper	Grow-through plant supports or stakes with twist ties	Some peppers are fine without support.
Pumpkin	Metal or wooden trellis with 7" (18cm) grid spacing	Use old T-shirts or pantyhose to sling fruit to the trellis as it ripens.
Summer squash	Metal or wooden trellis with 7" (18cm) grid spacing	Do not attempt to trellis bush varieties.
Tomato	Sturdy metal cage with 7" (18cm) grid spacing	See page 216 for how to make your own.
Watermelon	Metal or wooden trellis with 7" (18cm) grid spacing	Use old T-shirts or pantyhose to sling fruit to the trellis as it ripens.

Redwood posts and wire will support cane berries as they grow in.

but not into the compost bin unless you run a hot bin that heats up to more than 130°F (54.5°C), because anything less will not kill weed seeds or diseases.

Next, we get to disorderly. This means branches that are crossing, vines that have fallen away from trellises, berry canes that have become congested, or annuals that have gone to seed. Where to start?

Be Ruthless

If it won't be guided back to its trellis, cut it off. The other parts of the plant will most likely not suffer. In fact, they will probably be relieved of the burden and reward you with new, bushier growth. If annuals have gone to seed, pull them out (unless you plan to save seed from them). Those pyramid-shaped lettuces may look like they have plenty of succulent leaves left to eat, but by now they're bitter and not worth saving. Call a time of death and feed them to your compost bin.

Track Your Canes

This one requires thinking ahead, but if you can tie a ribbon to each berry cane that produces fruit, you will know exactly which ones to cut down to the ground at the end of the season. Blackberries and raspberries grow on second-year canes—canes that have been around for a year—and produce fruit the following season. Once they've

In small spaces, sometimes it's good to prune tomato suckers to keep the plant's size under control.

done so, it's time to cut those canes down. This trick will enable you to cut away spent canes while giving way to new growth for next year's harvest.

Tipping Is OK

It is perfectly acceptable, and even recommended, to cut watermelon and even squash vines if they are out of control. Count two leaf nodes past the fruit and cut or pinch off just beyond that second leaf. The vines can also be moved—if they're attached in only one place. Circle the vines around, back onto themselves.

Pinch Those Suckers

This isn't slang; it's the actual term used to describe new shoots that grow from the axil (where stem and leaflet joins) on tomato vines. If left unchecked, suckers will become branches with fruit all their own. What's wrong with that, you might ask? Suckers are named appropriately because they drain energy away from the fruit. After you have at least four trusses or clusters of fruit, start pinching suckers to help those tomatoes ripen as best they can. If you feel softhearted as you pull one off, know this: you can root it in soil and grow another entire tomato plant from it if you have room.

The exception is in climates with extreme summer temperatures, where you'll want to allow some suckers to grow. This provides extra leaf canopy to protect tomatoes from sun scald.

Pruning Cuts

There is one more bit of pruning information that will help you keep your garden in shape. It relates mostly to fruit trees but can apply to shrubs, hedges, and even some herbs. Knowing which type of pruning cut to use takes the mystery out of pruning. Let's look at the two options:

1. **Reduction cuts**—A reduction cut is used to trim a branch back from its tip. By cutting the branch just above a bud or leaf node on an angle, it triggers growth down along the branch. This cut causes a hormonal response. See, the leader tip naturally puts off a hormone called auxin, which prevents the other buds and leaves from becoming leaders themselves. When you cut away the tip of a plant, now the other buds and leaves can become larger branches. Reduction cuts help you fill in bare spots or create bushier hedges.

2. **Removal cuts**—This type of cut is used when you want to create more space. Remove a whole twig or branch by cutting it flush with another branch. You don't cut it above a bud, which would stimulate growth; instead, you cut it off at the shoulder, or the branch collar, as it's called. This is the type of cut you would use if you had branches of a fruit tree crossing in the center or touching one another. Choose which branch to keep, and cut the other one away.

* * *

Pruning is a huge subject, with variances for each plant. Find a good pruning class in your area and keep learning the skill until you feel confident. Some gardeners take classes each year in winter, just in time for winter pruning of fruit trees. Those regular reminders build confidence.

> ### GARDENING TIP:
> # PRUNE LIKE AN ARTIST
>
> **When you start pruning a shrub or vine, do what artists do: step back and look at your work occasionally. It will give you perspective on the overall shape, let you see what still needs to be cut away, and perhaps give you added courage to make additional necessary cuts.**

CHAPTER 9

Pest Control

Gardening is all rainbows and butterflies until your first head of lettuce is savagely snatched underground by a gopher, or your beautiful Swiss chard becomes ravaged by aphids overnight. Then, it's war. Some gardeners pull out the big guns: pesticides and biological warfare. But it doesn't have to be that way. This chapter gives you the tools to improve your odds against garden pests without reaching for heavy artillery. By using a multipronged approach, you'll spend most of your time enjoying the garden rather than pulling bottles of pesticides down from the shelf.

A ladybug hunts aphids on a Swiss chard leaf.

Best Practices for Organic Gardens

As we discussed in Chapter 1, by setting up your ecosystem to include a habitat for good bugs, utilizing regular crop rotation to discourage diseases and pest infestations, and planting a wide variety of crops, you will already be ahead of the pest-control game. Daily walks through the garden will also help keep you informed about your garden's predators. These steps are part of integrated pest management (IPM), a system used by organic farms all over the world. IPM also involves knowing something about the life cycle of the pests in your garden, so you can take steps to treat them at the right time. For example, if you know that grasshoppers lay their eggs in the soil to overwinter, you can unearth the eggs by lightly digging the soil during winter. You break the life cycle and drastically reduce your grasshopper problem in the garden. Here are a few other ways to ensure a safe growing environment for your plants.

Clear Diseased Plants

Diseased plant material left on the ground can foster another season of disease. Many afflictions, like blight and rust, live in the soil and come back year after year if plants are not disposed of properly. As mentioned earlier, don't compost any plants that have diseases unless you know your compost bin reaches 130°F (54.5°C). Lower temperatures don't kill powdery mildew or blight infestations, so play it safe and put those in your city's green waste bin. City municipal systems have the facilities to build large piles that get hot.

Keep Your Tools Clean

Diseases can spread from one branch to another on pruning shears. If you are pruning a diseased plant, dip the blades into a container of bleach or alcohol between cuttings. It may sound extreme, but it's the right thing to do to prevent the spread of many diseases. Clean your tools at the end of each season and disinfect them regularly with alcohol or bleach.

Use Natural Remedies First

The technique of hand-picking pests can go a long way in the garden. Simple garlic or pepper sprays, made by pureeing either garlic or pepper in a blender and adding a few drops of dish soap, will repel a number of pests. A layer of worm castings, with exoskeleton-dissolving chitinase, can solve many problems for you. Compost tea boosts plant vitality and inoculates your soil with beneficial microbes that interrupt the life cycles of many garden pests. Diatomaceous earth is another natural remedy that targets soft-bodied insects. It is a white powder made up of fossilized single-cell organisms. It feels like powder to us, but it's deadly to bugs. It pokes holes in bugs, which causes them to desiccate and die. Use a mask when applying. Be sure to reapply after rain or irrigation, because it becomes inert when wet.

✳ ✳ ✳

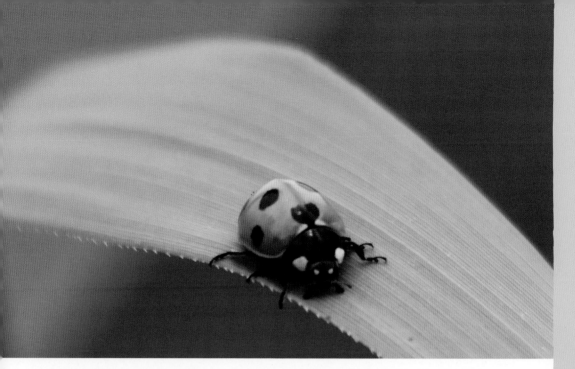

Attract lady beetles (ladybugs) to your garden by planting Umbelliferae flowers like yarrow, dill, cilantro, and alyssum.

By using these options first, you may never need to resort to over-the-counter horticultural oils or bug sprays. Note that even though USDA- or OMRI-certified organic sprays are safe for use in organic agriculture, some organic products are extremely strong and, just like their chemical counterparts, don't discriminate between beneficial insects and the ones you intend to exterminate.

In large-scale agriculture, walking the fields and hand-picking isn't feasible, so farms use sprays and other protections. In a home garden, however, it takes only a few minutes each day to assess the status of the garden and manage most pest problems without chemicals. One of the best ways to manage pests is by understanding them, so let's look at specific pests and their natural predators.

Good Bugs versus Bad Bugs

If you have pests in your garden, there is a good chance that those pests have enemies. Beneficial insects are the good bugs of the garden that eat or parasitize bad bugs. It's nature's way of balancing the equation. Following are some of the most helpful insects to include in your ecosystem.

- **Ladybugs (Coccinellidae family)**—Those cute beetles with red-and-black polka-dotted backs are voracious aphid eaters. Ladybug larvae consume about 400 aphids each as they grow into adults, so it's a good idea to attract them to the garden.

- **Lacewings (Chrysopidae family)**—These long green insects have transparent wings and long antennae. They eat aphids in addition to mites and other soft-bodied insects, as well as scale, which tend to infect citrus trees.
- **Hoverflies (Syrphidae family)**—Not to be mistaken for wasps, hoverflies (also called syrphid flies) have yellow-and-black striped bodies but are generally smaller and don't sting. Instead, they focus on eating aphids, thrips, leafhoppers, and mealy bugs. Hoverflies are also good pollinators.
- **Pirate bugs (Anthocoridae family)**—They don't wear patches over one eye, but they do scavenge the garden for bug booty. They are brown, long, and thin with piercing mouthparts, feeding on spider mites, thrips, aphids, some caterpillars (like corn and tobacco worms), whiteflies, scale, and potato leafhoppers.
- **Tachinid flies (Tachinidae family)**—Appearing similar to houseflies, these bulging-eyed bugs eat scale. They parasitize caterpillars, grasshoppers, and beetles.
- **Gall midges (Cecidomyiidae family)**—These tiny gnat-like creatures lay hundreds of eggs near aphids. The larvae inject a poison to first paralyze the aphids and then suck the life out of them, leaving a path of carcasses behind.
- **Parasitic wasps (Aphelinidae family)**—These are also tiny insects that manage aphids with ease. They can look like miniature flying scorpions when doing their job. They poke holes and lay eggs inside the pests. The aphids become hosts for young wasps. End of aphid story.

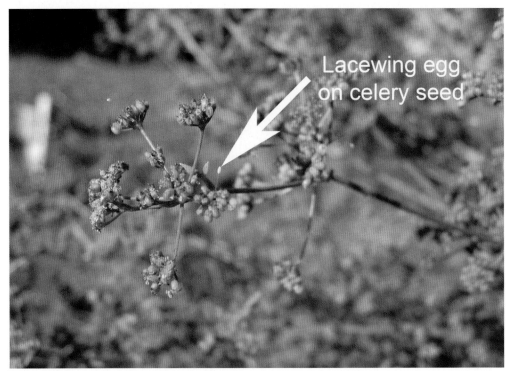

A lacewing egg sits atop a celery seedhead.

Lacewings eat aphids and other garden pests.

Tachinid flies are great predator insects to attract to your garden.

Decollate snails will bring your garden snail population back into balance.

- **Damsel bugs (Nabidae family)**—Commonly found in alfalfa fields, damsel bugs like to snack on caterpillars, leafhoppers, thrips, and aphids. They have a similar shape and coloring to pirate bugs.
- **Decollate snails (Achatinidae family)**—We've talked about the benefits of having toads, birds, bats, and bees in the garden, but there is one more creature to include in your arsenal of beneficial insects, though it is a gastropod, not an insect. These snails have conical-shaped shells and are cannibals—they eat the eggs and young of regular garden snails. Rather than attract these to your garden, you generally have to import them. Nurseries sell decollate snails in small containers right next to ladybugs and lacewings.

PESTS AND VANQUISHERS

Use this handy table to match the pest you have with the control solution.

BAD BUG	WHAT IT LOOKS LIKE	WHO EATS IT/ HOW TO GET RID OF IT
Ant	You saw them at your latest picnic	Ants provide a taxi service for aphids in exchange for the "honeydew" that aphids excrete. Control ants with borax traps, and aphids will decrease.
Aphid	Tiny, six-legged, with soft bodies that are all one color: either green, gray, black, or red	Ladybugs, lacewings, hoverflies, parasitic wasps, pirate bugs, and gall midges.
Cabbage worm/ moth	White butterflies that lay bright green worms on the undersides of cole crops	Birds, ground beetles, damsel and pirate bugs, tachinid flies, chickens, turkeys. Floating row covers decrease or prevent infestation.
Cutworm	Devious, earth-colored lumberjacks that mow down seedlings at soil level	See the sidebar on page 220.
Grasshopper	Green to brown leafhoppers up to 3" (7.5cm) in length	Kestrels, turkeys, rodents, reptiles, tachinid flies, and some spiders. Bird netting can be used in some cases.
Mealy bug	White, fuzzy, oval insects coated with powdery wax	Hoverflies, ladybugs, lacewings, parasitic wasps, and mealy bug destroyers. Feed plants with worm castings to repel them.
Scale	Typically light to dark brown, armored insects that seal themselves to branches and suck the life out of them	Lacewings, pirate bugs, ladybugs, parasitic wasps, tachinid flies, and mites. Horticultural oils suffocate scale. Hand removal works in small cases.
Snail and slug	Slimy, long bodies with stubby antennae, with or without shells	Birds, decollate snails, chickens, opossums, turkeys. Submerge shallow dishes of beer to soil level to trap; replace regularly.
Thrip	Thin, pointy-tipped insects with striped bodies	Lacewings, pirate bugs, predator thrips, parasitic wasps, and mites.
Whitefly	Small, winged, gnat-sized flies that occupy undersides of leaves, usually with powdery coating or concentric white circles	Ladybugs, lacewings, pirate bugs, parasitic wasps. Feed affected plants with worm castings to help repel insects.

Flowers for Battling Bugs

Now comes the fun part: figuring out how to attract beneficial insects to the garden. Most flowers attract pollinators, but certain flowers draw insect predators. With a little strategy and careful selection, you will increase your chances of ecological balance and tip the scales in your favor.

The table on page 181 shows the most common beneficial insectaries to plant in your garden. Choose at least three of these flower varieties to include in your garden—the more, the merrier. Plant them around the perimeter of raised beds or in the beds

Clockwise from top left: Cosmos, yarrow, and alyssum are all beneficial insectaries.

themselves. Tuck them into corners or plant them in pots nearby. Be prepared for your flowers to become a habitat for both good and bad bugs.

Floating Row Covers and Other Barriers

Beneficial insects aren't the only defense you have in the garden. Physical barriers are also part of a healthy garden. Protective coverings like homemade cloches (see Part 2) can mean the difference between survival and decimation for seedlings. Also, home gardeners and farmers use protective coverings to prevent pest infestations during critical periods of growth and to stave off frosty weather to extend the growing season. (Need a trick for preventing cutworm damage? See Part 2.)

Floating Row Cover and Garden Fabric

These are two names for the same thing: a lightweight, synthetic fabric that allows sunlight and water to pass through but keeps flying insects from landing on leaves

Lightweight floating row cover protects young seedlings from pests.

and laying their eggs on the undersides. It also keeps birds from pecking out newly planted seeds. Garden fabric is available in different degree of protection, from a summer-weight cover to an insulated frost blanket. Use U-pins to hold the fabric in place on top of the soil. Floating row cover can also be installed over hoops to create insulated tunnels along garden rows. Check under the fabric regularly for critters that may make it through the barrier.

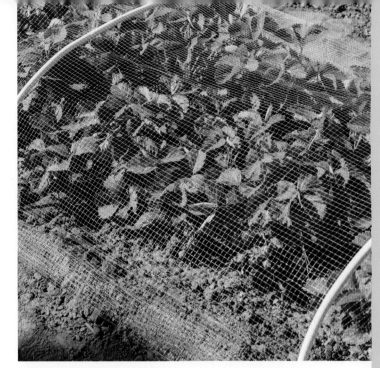

Cover tempting strawberries with low hoops and mesh netting to keep critters out.

Bird Netting

Bird netting is a nylon mesh with 1" (2.5cm) openings. It is perfect for covering crops that are regularly visited by rats, squirrels, and, of course, birds. Bird netting is nearly invisible and can be draped over strawberry patches, wrapped around fruit trees, and thrown over plants that are going to seed, keeping critters from invading. Netting is easy to lift for access to your crops or to replant a garden bed. Pin down the corners with U-pins to keep it from flying away in high winds.

Hardware Cloth

Some gardens need above-ground protection from larger invaders, like deer, goats, and neighborhood dogs. Hardware cloth serves this purpose and also provides below-ground protection. Hardware cloth is not really cloth; it is metal grid material that can be attached to the bottom of raised beds to prevent burrowing animals from stealing your root veggies. It is best added as the beds are being built. Staple the hardware cloth to the undersides (flip the beds over to accomplish this) or use screws with washers to ensure that the cloth is securely in place. Gophers can eat through chicken wire but are less likely to get through hardware cloth. Hardware cloth is worth the extra effort when planning a garden.

Walled Gardens

It may sound extreme, but for homes adjacent to wilderness, a walled or enclosed garden is the only option if you don't want to share your produce with the wildlife. A 3' (0.9m) wall is only tall enough to keep small critters out, but it's a good starting point. Deer have been known to leap 6' (1.8m) walls to sample delicious produce. You can build a decorative short wall and then line the outside of it with deer fencing (thick, 1" [2.5cm] mesh) that reaches a height of at least 8' (2.4m). The fencing will allow sunlight through and is less noticeable (in the same way that bird netting is less noticeable).

But that's not all: Dig a 3' (0.9m) deep trench around the garden and install hardware cloth vertically below ground along the fence. This will prevent burrowing animals from crossing under the fence. Sure, gophers can sometimes dig 6' (1.8m) down, but most travel only 2'–3' (0.6–0.9m) below the surface.

Walk-in Gardens

Some gardens require even more protection than an elaborate walled garden. If you have wild birds that swoop down to claim tomatoes as their own, or wild monkeys who come to visit frequently, you'll need a walk-in garden. It's basically a giant chicken or dog run for your vegetables. Use 2x4s to construct a frame and then cover the frame with hardware cloth—top to bottom, overhead and underground. The good news is that, with a walk-in garden, you can lock the door and you have unlimited trellis space—every part of the enclosure is a growing surface!

Fences are your friend when it comes to keeping out deer. They are worth the investment.

BENEFICIAL INSECTARIES FOR PEST CONTROL

WHAT TO PLANT	WHAT IT ATTRACTS	NOTES
CULINARY HERBS		
Caraway, cilantro, dill, fennel, parsley	Parasitic wasps, ladybugs, lacewings, hoverflies, and tachinid flies	Let them flower. These flowers are umbels, so their flowers form the shape of an umbrella. Umbels are generally a good choice for attracting beneficial insects.
Catnip, chamomile, chervil, mint	Parasitic wasps, hoverflies	Plant mint in its own pot to prevent it from overtaking your garden.
VEGETABLES (IF LEFT TO FLOWER)		
Carrot and parsnip	Parasitic wasps, ladybugs, lacewings, hoverflies and tachinid flies	See Caraway above.
Celery	Same as Carrot/Parsnip	Also an umbel when it flowers.
Cole crops and mustards	Ladybugs and other beneficials	Let them flower; they will attract aphids and, subsequently, good bugs.
FLOWERS		
Alyssum	Ladybugs, lacewings, parasitic wasps	Low-growing annual that reseeds itself.
Angelica	Lacewings	Also an umbel.
Calendula	Ladybugs, lacewings, hoverflies, bees	Repels many pests; can be brewed into a tea and used as bug spray.
Coreopsis	Parasitic wasps, hoverflies, and lacewings	Beautiful yellow flowers.
Cosmos	Parasitic wasps, hoverflies, and lacewings	Tall, wispy, pink or white flowers that reseed yearly.
Lupine	Gall midges, parasitic wasps, and hoverflies	In the legume family, so they also fix nitrogen in soils.
Marigold	Trap crop and repellent for many pests	Tuck these into corners of raised beds to protect vegetable crops.
Morning glory	Ladybugs and hoverflies	In some parts of the United States, this is considered an invasive plant.
Nasturtium	Trap crop for aphids	These are sprawling plants, so give them plenty of room.
Sunflower	Pirate bugs and parasitic wasps	Flowers produce seeds for birds or human consumption.
Yarrow	Parasitic wasps, hoverflies, and ladybugs	Perennial flower that is also an umbel.

So you walk out to the garden and find something wrong with your plants, but you don't know exactly what to do about it. You need a place to start. Here is a step-by-step flowchart to help you take action.

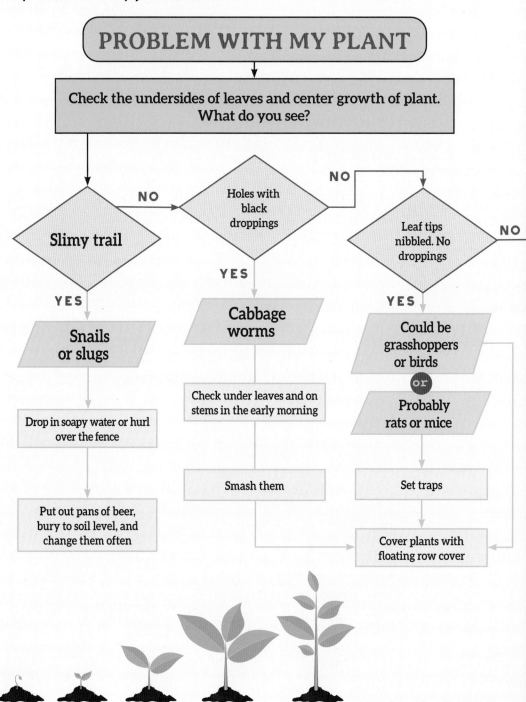

PROBLEM WITH MY PLANT

Check the undersides of leaves and center growth of plant. What do you see?

Slimy trail — NO →

Holes with black droppings — NO →

Leaf tips nibbled. No droppings — NO →

Slimy trail YES ↓
Snails or slugs
Drop in soapy water or hurl over the fence
Put out pans of beer, bury to soil level, and change them often

Holes with black droppings YES ↓
Cabbage worms
Check under leaves and on stems in the early morning
Smash them

Leaf tips nibbled. No droppings YES ↓
Could be grasshoppers or birds
or
Probably rats or mice
Set traps

Cover plants with floating row cover

Note: This flowchart covers the most common pest infestations but doesn't attempt to diagnose every issue. It also assumes that you know what aphids look like. The chart doesn't have an endpoint, which means that you may have to repeat the process for each pest issue several times. Keep in mind that gardening is not an exact science, and sometimes your best efforts may work, while other times they won't. Either way, it's best to take a deep breath and try again (eating ice cream helps, too).

CHAPTER 10

Now Pick It! (And Then What?)

This is the part of gardening that most people live for: when you get to eat what you've grown. There's nothing like sitting down to a homegrown salad with a colorful array of lettuces, mustard greens, arugula, radishes, and whatever else you like to throw into your salads. It almost doesn't need dressing; it's just that good. A homegrown tomato layered with fresh mozzarella, homegrown basil, olive oil, salt, and pepper is more and more satisfying with each bite. If grocery stores could capture the quality of this experience, we wouldn't need to garden, but there is no substitute for the flavors a home garden can bring to the table.

The joys of growing your own food come with the occasional moments of panic, when you harvest more zucchini, cucumbers, or basil than you know what to do with. This chapter aims to provide solutions for storing, preserving, and, yes, eating your harvest. It also offers a few simple recipes that answer the question, "Great, I grew this! Now what do I do with it?"

Slice or dice homegrown tomatoes to add color and unbeatable flavor to any meal.

Grow potatoes of different colors in the same bed to achieve a rainbow on your plate in no time.

Preparing Food for Storage

For a gardener, nothing stings more than spending all season growing your own food only to have it rot in the refrigerator. It happens all the time. That's why it's best to clean or prep veggies right when you bring them in from the garden. Some of these preparations go against what you might typically read about food storage, but they work.

Fill Up the Sink

Lettuces and other leafy greens will store for weeks if you soak them for twenty minutes in a sink or bowl full of water. Give them room to float around and stir them every once in a while. Soil and grime will sink to the bottom, and the plant cells will plump with water. Use a salad spinner to remove the excess water. Place a paper towel or small dishcloth at the bottom of a produce or plastic bag (hate to say it, but plastic bags work better than anything for this task), put your greens inside, and tie the bag closed. Store in the vegetable drawer of the refrigerator until ready to use. After this, salads are as easy as tearing individual leaves into a bowl. You can also go a step further and tear leaves into a large plastic or glass storage container, so all you have to do is put dressing on your greens when you're ready, but they don't last as long this way.

Store on the Counter or in the Pantry

Certain fruits and vegetables, including tomatoes, squash, avocados, melons, onions, and potatoes, should not be refrigerated. Stone fruits, such as nectarines, peaches, and plums, should be stored on the counter until ripe and then placed in the refrigerator drawer. Wash them just before eating.

Don't Wash Until Ready to Use

Some produce begins to decay quickly if you wash and store it: basil, beans, cucumbers, strawberries, and peppers. For these guys, brush off any soil and store in the fridge. Wash them right before you plan to use them.

Take Off the Tops

Carrots, radishes, and parsnips stay crisp longer if you take the greens off before putting them in the fridge.

Put Them in a Vase

Herbs such as cilantro, parsley, and even basil can be stored like flowers in a vase. If you put a plastic bag over the entire thing and store it on the top shelf in the refrigerator, replacing the water every few days, these herbs will last a long time. Some say asparagus can be stored this way too, though others prefer to store it in the fridge unwashed, wrapped in a paper towel in a plastic bag.

Use Magic Foil

When you wrap celery in a paper towel and then in aluminum foil, it lasts for a miraculously long time. Just don't forget about it.

Additional Tips

If possible, store veggies in clear containers. It is confusing to be greeted by unmarked bags of mystery produce when you open the vegetable drawer. Your food is more likely to be consumed when it's still fresh if you can clearly identify it. Many gardeners label their produce with sticky notes. There's no shame in that.

GARDENING TIP:
A SALAD SPINNER IS YOUR FRIEND

If you don't have a salad spinner, get one. It's a gardener's best friend when it comes to preparing produce for storage. The power of centrifugal force spins water off leafy greens, leaving them practically dry for storage. If you don't want to get a salad spinner, you can become one by wrapping your greens in a dish towel (gather up the corners), walking outside, and whirling your arm around like you're serving a softball game. Just make sure to stand away from anyone who doesn't like to get wet!

Blanching and Freezing

One of the best ways to preserve your harvest is to blanch and freeze it. It's easy to do and doesn't call for special equipment aside from a stockpot and a bowl of ice water. Let's look at the science behind the process.

Blanching is the act of placing vegetables in boiling water to scald them for a short period of time, usually between three and five minutes. During that time, enzymes—the ones that were hard at work to bring the food to ripeness—are killed. If left to continue, those enzymes would carry on ripening and degrading the color, flavor, and freshness of the food. Boiling water stops the process, essentially stopping time for your veggies.

BLANCHING/FREEZING TIMES

VEGETABLE	TIME
Asparagus	2 to 4 minutes
Beans	3 minutes
Beets	Cook through
Brassicas (broccoli, kohlrabi, collards, kale, but not cabbage)	3 to 5 minutes
Cabbages	1½ minutes
Corn (blanch before cutting from cob)	4 minutes
Peas	1½ to 3 minutes
Potatoes	3 to 5 minutes
Root crops (carrot, parsnip, turnip, but not beet), 1" (2.5cm) cubes	2 minutes
Squash, summer	2 to 3 minutes
Squash, winter	Cook through
Sweet potatoes	Cook through

The process is not complete, however, without the next step. Once boiling is finished, vegetables are plunged into an ice-water bath with temperatures below 60°F (15.5°C). The National Center for Home Food Preservation recommends 1 pound (450g) of ice for each pound (450g) of vegetables blanched. Place your vegetables in the ice bath for the same amount of time as they were boiled. For example, if you blanch green beans for three minutes, put them into the water bath for three minutes and then remove them.

Once cool, drain the vegetables and thoroughly pat them dry. This step is important because remaining moisture can cause ice crystals during freezing or otherwise damage the food. On this page is an at-a-glance chart of processing times for common vegetables. Use the shorter time for small or thin vegetables, and the longer time for thicker vegetables.

To freeze your blanched produce, place the vegetables in plastic bags, expel as much air as possible (air is the enemy!), and label the bags with the date and variety. Store them in the freezer and use them during the winter.

Peppers can be frozen whole without blanching. Just double-bag them to prevent freezer burn. Chop up frozen peppers for cooked dishes and stews.

Some vegetables and fruits freeze better if first frozen in a single layer on a cookie sheet and then collected into freezer bags for later use. Corn and peas will resist clumping if frozen on a tray first. Soft fruits, such as blackberries, blueberries, and raspberries, freeze best on a single tray, though they don't need to be blanched first, and apples and figs can be processed the same way. On a side note, frozen grapes are a terrific snack in the hot summer. Just put a cluster of fruit in the freezer and pop individual frozen grapes in your mouth when you need refreshment.

Drying/Dehydrating

Before the invention of refrigeration, dehydration was one of the most reliable means of preserving food. The process of dehydrating, as the name implies, removes water from fruits, vegetables, and meats. Without water, bacteria and fungi (in the form of yeasts and molds) cannot breed. The result is brittle, perfectly preserved, shelf-stable food that does not require refrigeration. It's a great solution for gardeners with very little freezer space, and, in some cases, the end product is better than its frozen counterpart.

There are several ways to dehydrate your harvest, including solar drying and electric dehydrators. From the simplest act of hanging a bundle of herbs upside down to dry in the garage, to the more elaborate contraptions like homemade solar food dryers (see Part 2 to make your own), dehydration is relatively straightforward and inexpensive to do at home. Let's look at the possibilities.

Air Drying

For simple herbs, such as sage, bay, thyme, oregano, dill, and rosemary, drying is as easy as spreading them out on a screen or paper towel in a room with plenty of air circulation. They may take up to a week to fully dry, but after they become brittle and crumbly, you can grind and store them in glass jars for use in savory dishes. You can also tie bundles of herbs with twine and hang them upside down to dry. These methods of drying should be done out of direct sunlight.

Electric Dehydration

Home-scale food dehydrators are readily available for the task if you're willing to spend the money. These enclosed units come with five to nine stacking trays and sit compactly on a kitchen counter. You simply load the trays, close the unit, and plug it in. Some dehydrators have timers, so you don't forget about your project and end up with unpalatable food-pebbles. Good-quality electric dehydrators will cost a couple hundred dollars, but loyal preservation folk will say it's worth the expense.

Oven Dehydration

Many gardeners and cooks use their ovens to dry their harvests on cookie sheets. The only caveat is that you must have an oven that can hold temperatures below 200°F (93°C). The ideal temperature for drying food is 140°F (60°C), although raw-foods advocates opt for temperatures below 115°F (46°C). Some ovens can accomplish this temperature with only the pilot light. If you have an electric oven that begins at 200°F (93°C), oven dehydration may not be an option for you.

FRUIT-DRYING TIPS

When it comes to drying fruit, other factors come into play. Commercial companies use sulfites to preserve color when drying, but home gardeners tend to shy away from preservatives. Instead, some soak fruit slices for five minutes in a mixture of vitamin C powder and water. Drying times vary, depending on the thickness and moisture content of the food.

The world of food preservation is immense, and this book doesn't venture to cover every trick of the trade. If you are new to dehydrating, there are plenty of in-depth dehydrating books out there. Check out the Bibliography and Resources section at the end of this book for a few suggestions.

GIVE THESE A TRY

Regardless of your chosen method of dehydration, it's a good idea to know which fruits and vegetables dehydrate the best. Here's a quick starter list of suitable crops to try:

VEGETABLES
- Bean
- Beet
- Carrot
- Corn, sweet and popping
- Garlic
- Mushroom
- Okra
- Onions (leek, green, bulb)
- Parsley
- Parsnip
- Peas
- Peppers, chili and sweet
- Potato
- Pumpkin
- Tomato
- Turnip
- Zucchini (sliced very thin)

FRUITS
- Apple
- Banana
- Blueberry
- Pear
- Stone fruits (apricots, peaches, plums)
- Strawberry

Solar Dehydration

Using the power of the sun to dry food is preferred by many gardeners because the sun's energy is free—there's nothing to plug in. It can be as simple as laying screens of food out on a table or rooftop and covering them with additional screens to keep the bugs away. You can go a step (or two) further by building a solar food dryer to harness the sun's power and incorporate convection, or consistent air current, into the mix. Learn how to make a solar food dryer in Part 2. Why convection? Because food dries faster with proper air circulation.

Electric dehydrators have fans to circulate air during the drying process, but the air is simply blasted over the surface of the food. Solar food dryers use convection—heat transfer by the circulation of fluids (in this case, air)—to speed the drying process. What would ordinarily take two days to dehydrate in an electric dehydrator can take only one day in a solar unit, depending upon its design.

You can preserve just a few jars at once without committing to big-batch canning.

Canning and Preserving

The practice of "putting up" the harvest has been a long-standing tradition among gardeners for hundreds of years. Its rise to household popularity, however, came about well after canning originated. The nineteenth-century French government offered a reward to anyone who could come up with a way of preserving war rations for the military. In 1809, Nicholas Appert, a brewer and confectioner, figured it out. He realized that sealed food didn't spoil, so he began developing a method to preserve food with heat in glass jars.

We've come a long way since then, but the basics of canning are still the same: the act of boiling closed jars of food kills any existing bacteria and seals the jars at the same time. After that, the food is shelf-stable. Once it's opened, the food is exposed to new bacteria and can begin to spoil, so it must be stored in the refrigerator.

The terms "canning" and "preserving" are often used interchangeably, but canning usually refers to savory foods or vegetables, while preserving is relegated to fruits (jams, jellies, marmalades, and the like). While this book does not endeavor to relay all of the nuances of canning, use this information as a jumping-off point to learn more about the process.

Start with Clean Jars

Run empty jars through the dishwasher or wash them in hot water and soap to remove dirt, dust, and hard-water deposits. Make sure that your jars are free of chips, bubbles, and cracks. Check each rim carefully, because a chip or crack in the rim can prevent proper sealing.

Next, place the jars in your canning pot and bring water to a boil. Your canning pot should come with a rack that keeps the jars from touching the bottom of the pot. Direct contact can cause the jars to crack, so if you don't have a rack, at least place a folded towel in the bottom of the pot, or improvise a rack by tying together extra canning-lid bands with string to place on the bottom of your pot—it's a quick homemade trivet!

Don't overcrowd the pot; leave space between jars to prevent them from coming in contact with each other. Boil them for 10 minutes (if you live above 1,000 feet [305m] elevation, add a minute for each additional 1,000 feet [305m]). Remove the jars with tongs and set them on dish towels. Now you're ready to fill them.

Prep the Lids

Most canning jars use screw-on metal bands and flat lids that have rubber gaskets. While the bands can be reused each year, you cannot reuse the lids. The rubber gasket is a one-time-use product. There are also glass or plastic alternatives to these traditional two-part lids that can be reused each year because they come with separate, replaceable rubber gaskets.

While your jars are boiling, prep your lids. Traditional lids are placed in warm water to soften the gaskets a few minutes before applying to the jars. Keep a pan of warm water on the stove with a pair of tongs (or a nifty canning-lid magnet) nearby for easy access to your lids once the jars are full and ready to be sealed.

WATER-BATH OR PRESSURE CANNING?

You might have noticed the previous mention of high-acid and low-acid foods. As it happens, the type of food you are preserving determines the method of preservation. Water-bath canning is possible with high-acid foods such as tomatoes, fruits, and pickles because they have a pH less than 4.6 or contain ample sugar or salt brine. Low-acid foods such as vegetables, meats, and dairy items require pressure canning to ensure a safe result.

Leave Some Headspace

Headspace is the amount of room between the surface of the food and the rim of the jar. You need to leave a certain amount of headspace in order to ensure a proper seal. Not leaving enough headspace means that your product can swell inside the jar and clog the seal. Too much headspace means that you might not get all of the air out during processing, which can encourage bacterial growth. Either way, you want to ensure the right amount of headspace: ¼" (0.5cm) for jams and jellies, ½" (1.25cm) for tomatoes and fruits (high-acid foods), and 1"–1¼" (2.5–3cm) for low-acid foods and meats.

Then What?

Once you remove your jars from boiling water, work quickly to fill them to the correct headspace. Use a spatula or chopstick to remove air bubbles from each jar and wipe the rims with a clean towel to remove any food residue before putting on lids and bands. This will increase your chances of a good seal. The band should be finger-tight or just tightened. This allows air to escape as the jars are processed and, later, as they cool. Avoid overtightening the jars; they could explode from the pressure created during processing.

Place the full jars back in the canning pot and return to a boil. Once a boil is reached, process for the proper time recommended in your recipe.

Remove the jars from the canning pot with the tongs and place them on a dish towel to cool. When a jar is properly sealed, you will hear a distinct "pop," and the lid will become concave. Master preservers recommend removing the bands before storage in order to reveal any hidden improperly sealed lids. Avoid stacking jars for the same reason.

GARDENING TIP:
BPA IN MY CANNING LIDS!?

Bisphenol A (BPA) is used to make many plastics in our world. It also happens to be an estrogen mimicker, which has been proven to wreak havoc on the human body. Sadly, BPA is found in many household products, from thermal paper receipts to the lining of canned foods to infant toys. While strides have been made to remove BPA from products, it remains as a coating on the inside of some major-brand canning lids. Those companies claim that their products contain FDA- and USDA-acceptable levels of BPA. For those who want to take back control, check out WECK glass-lid canning jars or do an online search for "reusable canning lids" for other sources.

Plan to grow yellow, red, orange, and black tomato varieties each year to increase diversity and color at the table.

Any jars that do not seal should be placed in the fridge and consumed first. Once the sealed jars have cooled, label them with the contents and date.

Use Trusted Recipes

While it's fun to experiment in the garden, canning isn't the time to jump headlong into trial and error. Use proven recipes or take a class to learn how to turn any canning recipe into a safe one. Contact your state university's Cooperative Extension Service to find out if they offer a Master Food Preserver program. Check out the next section for a trusted tomato canning recipe.

Eat It: Simple Recipes for Homegrown De-lish-es

The best cookbooks for gardeners are organized by vegetable rather than by salad, entree, and dessert categories. This section offers a selection of recipes that make the most of your abundant harvest of greens, squashes, root vegetables, and more. They are simple and delicious. After all, homegrown vegetables are best when prepared simply, not covered up with scads of sauces or buried under heavy flavors. These recipes are meant to highlight (or, if you prefer, showcase) the flavors of your garden—sometimes in ways you might not expect! Anyone can make them, and, best of all, each recipe either uses one pan or can be completed in under 30 minutes.

Impress your fellow gardeners with tasty garden specialties such as fresh pesto, home-canned tomatoes, roasted radishes, and more. Most of the following recipes have come either from family and friends or from experimentation based on trusted resources. The goal is to make it easy to use your harvest without much fanfare or work. Let's get started!

Garlicky Greens with Toasted Sesame Oil

Serves 2 to 3 as a side dish

This recipe comes from a fellow gardener, Carrie Manaugh from Ocean View Farms, Mar Vista, California. Use this with Swiss chard, kale, beet greens, and more mature mustard greens. You can use collard greens and cabbage too, but you'll need to cook them a little longer.

Ingredients

- 1 tablespoon extra-virgin olive oil
- 2 cloves garlic, minced or finely chopped
- 1 bunch (about 12oz [340g]) Swiss chard or any kind of kale, beet greens, collards, and the like), stems removed, roughly chopped
- 1 teaspoon tamari (I used Bragg Liquid Aminos)
- Toasted sesame oil

1. Heat the extra-virgin olive oil on medium heat in a large sauté pan. Add the garlic and stir for 1 minute. Don't let it start to brown.

2. Add the chard, drizzle with tamari, and stir to coat. Cook, stirring often for about 2 minutes. The chard will reduce in size but should not be completely wilted. If you want your greens softer, keep cooking for another 2 minutes.

3. Remove from the heat and drizzle with "a whiff" of toasted sesame oil. Stir to incorporate. Serve immediately with your favorite main dish.

Savory Winter Squash with Sage

Serves 2 to 3 as a side dish

There's no need to mask the savory goodness of winter squash with sugar. These earthy ingredients bring out the delicious flavors and natural sweetness. You'll never go back to sugary squash again.

Ingredients

- 1 winter squash—small pumpkin, kabocha, butternut, acorn, or delicata
- 1 shallot
- 1 tablespoon extra-virgin olive oil (use more for larger squash)
- 1 teaspoon rubbed sage
- Salt and pepper to taste
- ¼ cup (20g) shredded Parmigiano-Reggiano cheese*

* For a vegan recipe, leave out the cheese or use a vegan Parmesan substitute.

1. Preheat the oven to 400°F (204°C).

2. Peel pumpkins, butternut, and other squashes that have fibrous skins. Delicata and some acorn squashes can be eaten with skin on. Slice smaller squash into ½" (1.25cm) moons; slice larger squash into 1" (2.5cm) chunks. Cut the shallot into thin slices.

3. Add the squash and shallot slices to a 9" x 13" (23 x 33cm) baking dish. Drizzle with olive oil and toss with sage, salt, and pepper, using your fingers to coat all sides.

4. Bake in the oven for 10 minutes and then stir. Acorn- and delicata-type squashes, depending on size, may be finished after about 15–25 minutes total cooking time. More dense squashes, like pumpkin and butternut, will require more time. Cook those another 20–30 minutes, stirring occasionally, until the pieces can be pierced easily with a fork. If cooking different types together, put the squash that requires more cooking time in first and then add the quicker-cooking varieties as you go.

5. Remove from the oven and sprinkle with Parmigiano-Reggiano cheese or vegan substitute. Serve immediately.

Tender-Crisp Steamed Veggies with a Kick

Serves 2 to 3 as a side dish

Take your pick: this recipe works with broccoli, Romanesco, rapini, cauliflower, green beans, or peas. It's based on a tasty discovery in Dr. Andrew Weil's *8 Weeks to Optimum Health*.

Ingredients

- 1 head broccoli or 8oz (225g) green beans/sugar snap peas/snow peas, rinsed and drained, trimmed as needed
- 1 clove garlic, thinly sliced
- ¼ cup (60mL) water (½ cup [120mL] for beans and cauliflower)
- 1 teaspoon extra-virgin olive oil
- Salt and pepper to taste
- Pinch of red pepper flakes

1. Break or cut the florets into bite-sized pieces. Peel and chop the stem into ½" (1.25cm) chunks.

2. Place the pieces in a pan with a tight-fitting lid large enough to accommodate your chosen vegetable. Add the garlic slices. Pour water over the vegetables and then drizzle with olive oil. Sprinkle with salt and pepper and red pepper flakes.

3. Put the lid on the pan and bring the water to a boil. Watch and listen closely. When it boils, reduce to a low simmer and cook, covered, no more than 5 minutes (for beans and cauliflower, add 5–7 minutes). Turn off the heat and drain remaining liquid. Serve while the gettin's good.

Sesame-Roasted Radishes

Serves 2 to 3 as a side dish

Radishes have a very distinct flavor when raw; to some gardeners, that flavor only goes so far. Once you roast them, though, they transform into something completely different. If you were ever on the fence about growing radishes, this recipe will nudge you over. It's a riff on one part of a recipe from Jamie Oliver. Try it with turnips too!

Ingredients

- 1 pound (450g) radishes, greens removed
- 1 tablespoon walnut or peanut oil
- 1 green onion, chopped
- 1 tablespoon tamari
- Toasted sesame oil
- Furikake, gomashio, or sesame seeds (I used Eden Shake)

1. Preheat the oven to 375°F (191°C).

2. Trim the radishes and cut them into quarters. Place them in a casserole dish and toss with walnut oil. Roast until the radishes are tender and starting to brown, about 25 minutes.

3. Remove from the oven and add the green onion and tamari. Stir to coat and then return to the oven for 5 more minutes. Test for doneness—the radishes should be easily pierced with a fork.

4. Remove from the oven and drizzle lightly with toasted sesame oil. Sprinkle furikake over the top and serve warm.

Romantic Notions of Roasted Vegetables

Serves 2 to 3

You can play around with using carrots, parsnips, turnips, and even potatoes and sweet potatoes here. Throw in eggplant or kohlrabi (cooks like potatoes) to see what happens. Beets have strong flavors, so fair warning—they will influence the overall flavor. Vegetables that take longer to cook are cut into smaller dice, so everything ends up cooking evenly. Eggplant is cut larger, so it doesn't get soggy. Halloumi is a Greek cheese that browns and holds its shape when grilled. It's wonderfully salty and elevates this dish to the next level. Throw in some kale and you've got a great meal.

Ingredients

- 1 eggplant, cut into 1½" (3.75cm) chunks
- 2 to 3 parsnips (5oz [142g]) cut into ½" (1.25cm) cubes
- 1 to 2 carrots (5oz [142g]) cut into ¾" (2cm) cubes
- 1 kohlrabi, peeled and cut into ½" (1.25cm) cubes

- 1 tablespoon fresh parsley (or 1 teaspoon dried)
- 1 tablespoon fresh oregano (or 1 teaspoon dried)
- 7 teaspoons extra-virgin olive oil, divided
- Salt and pepper to taste

- 3oz (85g) Halloumi cheese, cut into ½" (1.25cm) cubes (optional)
- 5 kale leaves, stems removed
- ⅛ teaspoon garlic powder

1. Preheat the oven to 400°F (204°C).

2. Chop the vegetables as noted; rough chunks are perfect for this dish. Place the first four ingredients in a 9" x 13" (23 x 33cm) roasting pan. Sprinkle with parsley and oregano and then drizzle with about 2 tablespoons olive oil. Add salt and pepper and then toss the ingredients to coat. Bake 15 minutes.

3. While the vegetables are roasting, prepare the Halloumi cheese, if using. When the timer goes off, add the Halloumi to the roasting pan, stir, and return to the oven for another 15 minutes.

4. Chop the kale leaves into 1" (2.5cm) wide strips and place in a bowl. Drizzle with 1 teaspoon olive oil and sprinkle with garlic powder. Massage the oil into the kale.

5. In the last 5 minutes of cooking, test the vegetables for doneness. They should be pierced easily with a fork. Add the kale to the roasting pan and finish cooking. The kale should be cooked, with a few crisp edges.

Crispy (Addictive) Kale Chips

Serves 4

"What are kale chips?" That's usually the question when a bowl of oven-crisped kale is put down in front of a newbie. The person eats one out of curiosity and is surprised to find that kale can taste so good. That's all it takes to get hooked. Try not to eat them all at one sitting, or at least share with friends!

Ingredients

- 12oz (340g) kale, stems removed (curly kale works best, but you can use several varieties for diversity)
- 1 tablespoon extra-virgin olive oil
- 1 tablespoon apple cider vinegar
- ⅛ cup (8g) nutritional yeast (or more to taste)
- Salt to taste

1. Preheat the oven to 300°F (149°C).

2. Tear the kale into 3" (7.5cm) pieces (they shrink). In a large bowl, combine the kale, olive oil, and apple cider vinegar. Use your hands to massage the leaves until coated evenly. Sprinkle with nutritional yeast and salt and toss to combine.

3. Place the leaves in a single layer on two baking sheets. Bake in batches for 15–17 minutes until crisp, rotating trays halfway through. Curly kale takes longer than lacinato (dinosaur) kale.

David King's Pesto-Madness Pesto

Makes about 4 cups (1L)

When you have more basil than you know what to do with, you make pesto. It freezes well and captures the unforgettable flavor of summer. David King, the former garden master at the Learning Garden in Mar Vista, California, developed this pesto recipe over years of delicious trial and error.

Ingredients

- 8 cloves garlic
- ¾ cup (168g) toasted pine nuts
- 8 cups (192g) fresh basil leaves, loosely packed
- 1⅔ cups (167g) Parmesan cheese
- 2 teaspoons fresh black pepper
- 1⅓ cups (315mL) olive oil

1. Add the garlic, pine nuts, basil, cheese, and black pepper to a food processor or high-speed blender and pulse to combine. Add the olive oil and process just until a puree forms, or process longer for smooth pesto. Scrape down the sides as needed.

2. Use immediately or store in sealed containers with a little extra olive oil on top. The oil will help prevent discoloration. Pesto can be frozen in ice cube trays or single containers. Yummy!

The jars of canned tomatoes sit undisturbed overnight.

How to Can Tomatoes

1 pound (450g) tomatoes makes approx. 3 pints (1.4L)

My mother, Jo Wilhelmi, has always been known for her tomato sauce. It's what brought friends over for dinner. Every batch started with tomatoes that she had canned the summer before. She may not have grown them herself, but she went to a local farm and picked every one of them off the vine. With eyes bigger than common sense allowed, we always ended up with about 100 pounds (45kg) more than we anticipated picking. Naturally, the only solution was to can them all. This recipe comes from her Italian grandmother, Antonia, and can be used to make 3 to 300 jars, and it is best done with friends.

Ingredients
- Fresh tomatoes (at least 1 pound [450g])

Equipment
- Water bath or large stockpot
- Colander
- Sterilized jars, bands, and new lids
- Small saucepan for warming lids
- Tongs
- Dish towels

1. Place the washed tomatoes in a large bowl; pour boiling water over the tomatoes. Take the tomatoes out of the water within a minute and remove the skins (scoring them beforehand makes it even easier).

2. Cut the tomatoes in halves or quarters and squeeze out most of the seeds. Place the tomatoes in a colander as you peel the rest.

3. Pack the tomatoes in jars as tightly as possible with a little juice on top (this occurs naturally). Remove air bubbles with a plastic knife, thin spatula, or chopstick. Leave a ½" (1.25cm) headspace. Wipe the rim of each jar.

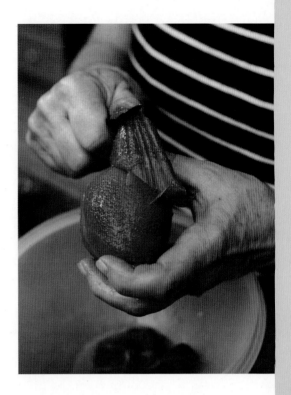

4. To prepare the lids, boil water in a small saucepan.

5. Turn off the heat and place the lids in the hot water for about 3 minutes. Remove a lid with tongs and place it on a sterilized jar, making sure the surface is clean. Screw the cap on but do not tighten too much.

6. Place a cloth on the bottom of a large stockpot or use a canning rack, and put the filled jars in the pot. Fill with water to cover the lids, bring to a boil, and boil covered, slowly, for 30 minutes only.

7. Turn off the heat, uncover the stockpot, and let the jars sit for about 10 minutes longer in the water. Using tongs, take the jars out and place them on a dish towel. Leave them undisturbed for 12 hours. The next morning, the jars should be sealed (the center of each lid shouldn't move or click when you press on it). If any jars did not seal properly, store them in the refrigerator and use within the next week.

PART 2: DIY Projects for a Productive Garden

In this section, you'll find step-by-step instructions to build that raised bed, create that irrigation system, and so much more. Want to start composting? Need to build a trellis for your tomatoes? It's all here in Part 2. Tackle a project now or save a project for later. Either way, you have the resources you need in these pages to design and build the small-space garden of your dreams. You'll be glad you took the time to follow these steps.

Don't worry, you don't need to be a carpenter or contractor to make these projects. Some only require a calculator or a little elbow grease. These projects include tricks that help you protect your crops, save and store seeds, start a worm bin or compost pile, and a few other fun things. This is where we get down to details of how to build raised beds that will last, calculate soil volume to fill those beds, and set up an easy and efficient drip-irrigation system. Whether you are taking the traditional gardening path or exploring more regenerative practices, you'll feel more confident as you read the instructions and work your way through the DIY section that follows. Take it one step at a time. Soon you'll be enjoying the benefits of a home-grown garden.

Raised-Bed Building Tips

There are many ways to build a raised bed, from *Sunset Magazine*'s basic structure (*sunset.com/garden/perfect-raised-bed*) to less formal beds made from recycled fencing. *Sunset*'s raised bed uses corner posts, but some gardeners prefer to reclaim those precious inches of growing space taken up by posts and build their beds without them. Either way, if you build your bed with materials that last, using the helpful tips offered here, you will be able to enjoy your raised beds for years to come.

- **Build on a level surface**—It seems like a no-brainer, but you'd be surprised how many people try to assemble their raised beds in the garden among the foliage. Do yourself a favor and build the beds on a concrete patio or another level surface and then move them into place.

- **Use deck screws**—It will save you time (and maybe even a trip to the emergency room) to use 3" (7.5cm) galvanized deck screws or stainless steel screws instead of nails. Predrill your holes if you are working with materials like Trex decking, which splits easily near the ends.

- **Put the ugly side in**—Lumber has an ugly side. It always does. Whether it's a knot, a crack, or the neon-orange spray paint the company used to mark the product, you are likely to find flaws in the wood. Be sure to situate that flawed surface toward the inside of the raised bed, where the soil can cover it. While you're at it, check the wood for splinters or rough edges and point the roughest edge to the ground. This saves you the time and effort later on of either pulling splinters out of your thumb or sanding down your new bed.

- **Hardware cloth, not chicken wire**—If you have burrowing animals in your neighborhood, there is one important step to take as you build your beds: line the

bottoms securely with hardware cloth (welded wire mesh). Chicken wire is thin, and gophers can chew through it, but ½" (1.25cm) hardware cloth will last for years and put your concerns to rest before you've even added soil to the beds.

Raised beds give plants more room to grow and mean you have to bend down less.

TRY A KEYHOLE GARDEN

A keyhole garden uses permaculture design principles that aspire to create more edges in the garden. The more edges you create, the more planting surface you have. This design is based on the shape of a keyhole and can be built as a waist-high raised bed or as low as a few inches (7 or 8cm) above ground. Think of it as a circle with a pathway leading into the center from one edge. The circle is 8'–12' (2.4–3.7m) in diameter. The entire area of the circle is planted, but not the pathway. Gardeners access the garden space from the center of the circle, along the pathway, and along the outer circumference of the circle.

Some keyhole gardens incorporate a compost pile into the center of the circle. If you try this option, make sure that your planting area is narrow enough so that you can reach it entirely from the outside of the circle. Keyhole gardens are an efficient use of space and break the straight-line boundaries of formal raised beds.

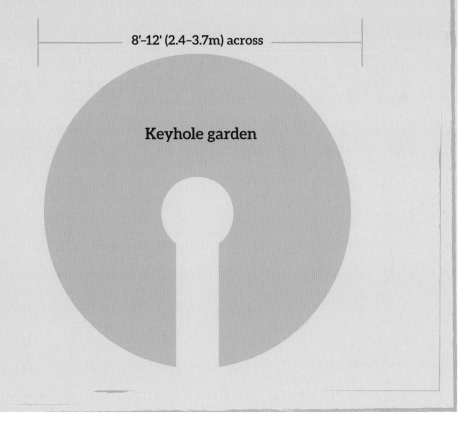

8'-12' (2.4–3.7m) across

Keyhole garden

How to Build a Raised Bed

1. Cut pieces of 2" x 12" (5 x 30.5cm) lumber to the appropriate size. For a 4' x 8' (1.2 x 2.4m) raised bed, purchase three 8' (2.4m) pieces of lumber, and then you will only have to cut one board in half. Your beds will have an external dimension of 4' x 8' (1.2 x 2.4m), but your internal dimensions, the actual growing area, will be slightly smaller.

2. Align the pieces vertically and bring the corners together as shown (see the diagram on page XX) on a level surface. Predrill the holes as needed and connect the corners with three 3" (7.5cm) deck screws per side.

3. Once the frame is assembled, flip the bed over and attach hardware cloth to the bottom edge (if you are using hardware cloth) with ½" (1.25cm) construction staples. Return the bed to the correct side and position it in the garden.

4. Check the bed with a level to ensure that the foundation is level. If your bed is sloped, water is likely to drain unevenly, and you may experience pooling in low areas.

5. Use a mallet or hammer to insert the 18" (46cm) predrilled flat steel stakes against the inside walls of the raised bed. Place the stakes 2' (61cm) apart. These prevent the wood from twisting or bowing under the weight of wet soil. It also prevents the bed from shifting over time, especially if you are building taller beds with several layers of wood. You will need to adjust the length dimensions of the stakes if you build taller beds. For a 12" (30.5cm) bed, 18" (46cm) stakes are appropriate. Hammer the stakes into the ground so that the top end of the stake sits about 1"–2" (2.5–5cm) below the top edge of the raised bed. You will not be able to see the stakes once the bed is filled with soil.

6. Secure each stake to the wood frame with four 1½" (3.75cm) wood screws as shown (see "Metal stake placement inside front view" on the diagram). If you plan to attach a sitting rail or cap to the top edge of your raised bed, this is the time to do it.

7. Congratulations! Now you are ready to fill your bed with soil.

8. If you don't have enough existing soil and compost to fill your raised beds, you will need to start off with bagged nursery planting mix, bulk organic vegetable garden soil, or a combination of ingredients. Once the beds are established, regular composting will keep you supplied with soil amendments.

Raised Bed Assembly

Place stakes every 2' (61cm)

3" (7.5cm) deck screws

Bed assembly top view

Soil level

1½" (3.75cm) screws

Metal stake placement inside front view

3" (7.5cm) deck screws

Bed assembly front view

A Formula for New Raised-Bed Soil

Before we get started, let's get something straight: there's no actual soil in potting soil. It's a misnomer. Potting soil is usually made up of decomposed organic matter, like compost, wood chips, lumberyard waste, and peat moss. It also has perlite—that white puffy stuff that looks and sounds like Styrofoam when you crush it. Perlite is puffed volcanic glass that allows water to flow better through the soil medium. It doesn't hold nutrients or add nourishment to the plants. It's simply there as a placeholder for air and water.

Peat moss is widely used in potting soils to hold moisture and improve soil texture. It is acidic and can help adjust alkaline pH when needed. The trouble is that peat moss is a natural resource that is being depleted around the world. It takes about 3,000 years for nature to make a peat bog, and we're using it up faster than it can reproduce. As an alternative, some forward-thinking soil companies are starting to incorporate a peat moss substitute into their potting soils instead. That alternative is called *coir*. It's mispronounced by most, but the correct pronunciation (in English, anyway) is "coy-yer." Coir works like peat to hold moisture and improve soil texture, but it's made from a waste product, so it's renewable.

Coir is made from the outside hull of coconuts—the part that is thrown away. The raw product has a high salinity, so it must be thoroughly rinsed before use. Thankfully, most manufacturers producing coir for the hydroponics industry are meticulous in eliminating salts before packaging the product. Investigate your provider before using a new material and inquire with your nursery professional about carrying coir-based products for your neighborhood.

That bag of potting soil from the store will probably say "organic," but know this: there is no regulation about the use of the word *organic* in soil amendments. When we go to the grocery store and buy organic produce, we know it has been grown without pesticides and chemical fertilizers according to United States Department of Agriculture (USDA) organic standards. In the world of soil amendments, *organic* simply means "of, relating to, or derived from living matter." Keep this in mind as you read about fertilizers as well.

Now that you have an idea of what's in those bags, let's talk about how to make your own raised-bed planting mix. Here's the formula: start with 50% compost, 40% coir, and 10% perlite or vermiculite, depending on your existing soil conditions. Vermiculite does the opposite of perlite. It is a puffed mineral that is exploded like popcorn. It holds water like a sponge, which helps sandy soils retain moisture. It doesn't break down, so you need to apply it only once. Vermiculite has a checkered past: at one point, a major mining source discovered that their vermiculite was contaminated with asbestos, but OMRI (Organic Materials Review Institute) put regulations into practice to ensure that each batch is now certified asbestos-free before sale.

You can also throw in coffee grounds and organic fertilizer if you like. This is just a starting point, however. If you mix in some of your existing soil, you will want to adjust the percentages a bit. If you have clay soil, add more compost to break up tight particles. If you have sandy soil, use more coir to hold moisture better. Play around with this. It's all part of the experiment of gardening.

Now, to calculate your soil needs (for amounts using metrics, see page 214). If you have a raised bed that is 12" tall, it will be easy to figure out how much planting medium you will need. It's simply length x width x 1 = cubic feet (because your bed is 1' tall). If you have a shorter raised bed, you will need to do a little more math: length x width x height, but this time the height will be a fraction of 1'. For example, let's say you have a bed that is 4' wide, 6' long, and 8" tall. First, multiply 4' x 6' to get 24'. Then divide 12" into 8" to get 0.667 (this is the fraction of 1'). Multiply 24' x 0.667 to get 16 cubic feet of soil. If your bed is 10" tall, use 0.834 for the height; if it is 6" tall, use 0.5 for the height.

Volume = 4' x 6' x (8"/12") = 16 cubic feet
(or 4 feet x 6 feet x 0.667 feet = 16 cubic feet)

Once you have figured out the cubic footage, multiply that total by 50% to find out how much compost you need. Then multiply the cubic footage total by 40% for how much coir, and then by 10% for perlite. For example:

Our bed needs 16 cubic feet of soil.

50% of 16 is 8 cubic feet of compost.

40% of 16 is 6.4 cubic feet of coir.

10% of 16 is 1.6 cubic feet of perlite.

Most bags of nursery potting soil and compost are sold in quantities of either 1.5 or 2 cubic feet (42 or 56L). Divide your totals for each material by the bag size you plan to buy, and that will tell you how many bags to load into your car.

SOIL FORMULA IN CUBIC METERS

The formula here is the same: length x width x height = cubic meters. Since soil is not typically sold in cubic meters but liters, we'll do one more step to find that measurement.

Let's use the same amount from the example on page 213, where the bed is 1.2m wide, 1.8m long, and 20.3cm tall. First, multiply 1.2m x 1.8m to get 2.2m. Then divide 100cm into 20.3cm to get 0.2 (this is a fraction of 1m). Multiply 2.2m x 0.2 to get 0.4 cubic meters. Multiply 0.4 by 1000 to get 400L of soil.

Volume = 1.2m x 1.8m x (20.3cm/100cm) x 1000 = 400L

(or 1.2 meters x 1.8 meters x 0.2 meters x 1000 = 400 liters).

For the breakdown of each soil component in this example:

50% of 400 is 200L of compost.

40% of 400 is 160L of coir.

10% of 400 is 40L of perlite.

Potting soil is a mixture of compost, coir, and perlite, which you can combine yourself for a lower cost.

Calculation of Precipitation Rate (PR) of Drip Emitters
by Russell Ackerman, CLIA-D

Water typically infiltrates into soil at a rate of ¾" (2cm) per hour or less. By slowing the rate at which water is applied to a landscape, we can prevent runoff and allow water to percolate through the soil, down to the plant roots where it's needed.

Precipitation Rate (PR)—The rate at which water is applied to a landscape area by an irrigation system or watering device measured in inches per hour.

Total Root Area—The total square footage of soil above the mature root systems of all irrigated plants in the zone.

Total Zone GPM—The total amount of water applied by all of the emitters in the zone in gallons per minute.

GPH—Gallons per hour (÷ 60 min/hr to get gallons per minute) [**Author's note:** Drip tubing is rated by gallons per hour, so a product that says 0.5 indicates that the emitter flow rate is 0.5 GPH.]

231.1—A conversion factor that converts gallon/hour to cubic inches/hour.

Formula: PR = (231.1 x Emitter Flow Rate in GPH) ÷ (Emitter Spacing in inches x Row Spacing in inches)

Example: Backyard with rows of Rain Bird XF 0.5 x 12" tubing spaced 15" apart.
(231.1 x 0.5) ÷ (12 x 15) = 115.6 ÷ 180 = 0.64 in/hr—0.64 < 0.75 in/hr = good!

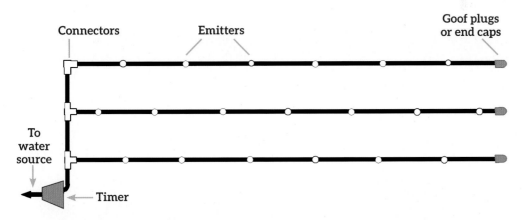

A reliable drip system using ½" (13mm) tubing, tee connectors, and end caps (use goof plugs for ¼" [6mm] tubing).

Homemade Tomato Cages:
How to Build a Tomato Crib

What the heck is a tomato crib, you ask? Well, for starters, it involves breaking a rule—or, at any rate, a commonly held belief—about tomato growing. Most nurseries and gardening books will tell you that you have to space tomato plants 2'–3' (0.6–0.9m) apart. This tomato crib allows you to grow four different varieties of tomatoes in 4 sq ft (0.4 sq m) of space without wrestling with round, weak tomato cages. If you prepare your soil correctly, you will have a bounty of tomatoes that will have your neighbors either welcoming or dreading your knock on their door (depending on how much they like tomatoes).

After you've prepared your soil for planting (mixed in organic fertilizer for acid-loving plants and added plenty of compost because tomatoes are considered "heavy feeders," meaning that they need a lot of nutrients to draw upon), follow these instructions.

First, let's plant your tomatoes. Mark out an area 1' (30.5cm) wide x 4' (122cm) long and divide the space into four equal squares. Mark the center of each square. Dig a hole for each tomato plant that is twice as deep as the root ball.

Snip or pinch off all the leaves from the base of the plant up to the level that is equal to a few inches (7–8cm) above the surface of the planting hole. This will accomplish two things: (1) deep roots mean strong plants, and (2) trimming the leaves will keep water and soil from accumulating on your plant leaves.

Next, throw a handful of Epsom salts into each hole. This will help prevent

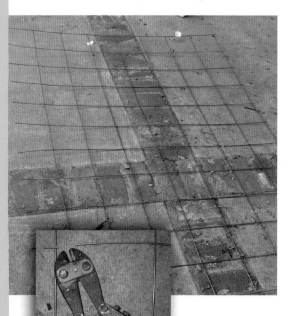

blossom-end rot, a nasty disease that ruins otherwise perfectly good tomatoes, come harvest time. Mix that in and plant each tomato, backfilling it gently (don't push down; let watering do the work for you, and then you can add more soil).

Now, once your tomatoes are planted, you will need a 10' (3m) length of concrete wire mesh (the kind that stands up on its own) that is 5' (1.5m) tall, with generous 6" x 6" (15 x 15cm) grid spacing so you can get your hands through when harvesting. Use wire cutters to cut the horizontals off one edge of the mesh to expose vertical spikes that will be your anchors that drive into the ground.

Cut the metal mesh to the size you need.

Next, it's time to make a 1' x 4' (30.5 x 122cm) rectangular cage by making 90-degree folds in the width of the fencing at the 1' (30.5cm) mark, the 5' (1.5m) mark, and the 9' (2.75m) mark. The photograph at right shows the result.

Connect the ends of the fencing together to form the box and then tie them closed with wire. Now you have a crib to put around your tomatoes. Position the box over your tomatoes and watch them grow. You're almost finished.

As your tomatoes grow taller, weave sturdy twine across the opening of the crib to create a grid for the tomatoes to grow through. Start by tying off the twine near a corner, and run it across the cage to wrap it around the other end of the wire mesh. Then take the twine to the next rung, wrap it once around that rung, and continue directly across to the other side. Continue running twine around each rung and across to the opposite side until you've covered the opening, and then weave twine perpendicularly through to complete the grid.

Start near the bottom and work your way up. Usually, you will want to add a new layer of twine per week as the tomatoes grow through

Once installed, the tomato crib will train the plants to weave upward.

Tomato crib lattice allows you to look down into the inside of a tomato crib.

the lower layers of twine. It takes only a few minutes to add a new layer. Within about a month, you will have created a three-dimensional lattice that cradles your tomato vines, and you won't have to worry about them for the rest of the summer.

See page 218 for diagrammed instructions to make a tomato crib that holds eight tomatoes (a 2' x 4' [61 x 122cm] cage).

How to Build an Eight-Plant Tomato Crib

These instructions are similar to those for the four-plant tomato crib. This one is just twice as wide to allow for two rows of tomatoes instead of one. These illustrations also demonstrate how to weave twine for the grow-through trellis.

Plant your tomatoes and situate the crib over them. Next, you're ready to start weaving twine to support your tomatoes as shown on the opposite page.

As weeks progress and your tomatoes grow, add another layer of lattice above the first one. Repeat each week until the entire crib is filled in.

A 12' (3.7m) length of concrete wire mesh is folded at points A to D as noted. Don't forget to use wire cutters to remove the horizontals from one edge of the mesh to expose vertical spikes, which will be your anchors that drive into the ground.

When folding is complete, it looks like this from the top.

Connect the ends and secure closed with wire. The tomato crib should stand up on its own, with spikes pointing into the soil.

Start at the bottom of one end and weave a lattice across the interior of the crib. String twine along the X axis and then run perpendicular twine across the Y axis to complete the lattice.

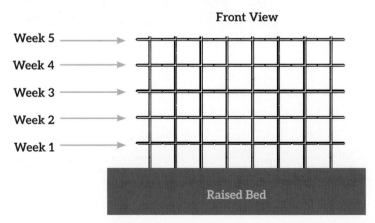

Tomatoes will get support from the very beginning as they grow to fill in the crib. Adding twine each week is easy to do and will help train your tomatoes to grow straight up through the lattice.

GARDENING TIP:
PREVENTING CUTWORMS

Cutworms are pests that strike at night, when you least expect it. They live in the soil and then surface when it's dark to mow down your seedlings to nubs. Toilet paper rolls or paper towel rolls—cut into 2" (5cm) lengths—can solve the problem in most cases. Right after planting, shimmy a cardboard collar into place around your seedling and twist it partway into the soil to block cutworms from accessing your plants. If they attack your garden unprotected, dig gently around the damaged area to locate the culprit curled up in the soil; cutworms don't travel far from the scene of the crime.

Cut cardboard tubes into 2" (5cm) lengths, which should be enough to prevent cutworms.

These tubes can stay from sprout stage to full-grown plant.

Homemade Cloche aka Mini-Greenhouse

Nothing keeps your direct-seeded babies safer from bugs and cold better than their own mini-greenhouse, or cloche, as it's called by the French (pronounced like "close" with "sh" at the end instead). Traditional glass cloches, like the kind used in French intensive gardening, can be prohibitively expensive and often do nothing to protect plants from cutworms. A simple solution that also happens to be a great recycling project is to make mini-cloches from your used plastic water bottles. These offer more protection than traditional cloches. Here's how:

Remove the cap and ring from a bottle and lay the bottle down horizontally. With a sharp box-cutter or mat knife on a solid surface, cut the bottle in two by inserting the knife halfway between the top and bottom and working your way around the bottle, rotating away from you as you go. When you have finished, you will have two halves. The top half is ready to use right away; the bottom half needs one more thing: a ventilation hole. Turn the bottom half of the bottle upside (cut side) down. Insert the knife into the top surface and cut out a flap or triangle. Now your plants can get some air and you will be able to water directly through the hole in the cloche. Note: For taller seedlings, like green onions or carrots, just cut the bottoms off your bottles, and you will have tall cloches in an instant.

Mini-greenhouses protect sprouts and seedlings.

In your garden, use cloches to cover your seedlings as they emerge from the soil. Push the cloche down into the soil with a twist to create a barrier around the plant both above and below ground. This will keep all sorts of pests at bay: sow bugs (roly-polies), cutworms, snails, slugs, and grasshoppers. When plants have two sets of true leaves, or they outgrow the cover, remove the cloches. When the cloches lose their shape, toss them in the recycling bin. Use 8-ounce bottles for small plants (lettuces, green onions, flowers) and 1-L bottles for wider plants (zucchini and other squash).

Seed Storage the Gardenerd Way

Seeds are wonderful things. They contain all the genetic information they need to germinate and grow into food-producing plants. With a little help from you, adding soil and nutrients to the mix, seeds will thrive and reward your efforts with fresh fruit, abundant greens, and delicious vegetables for several months. It all starts with viable seed. We will discuss doing a germination test on the opposite page, but here are tricks to storing seeds so your germination rates are higher. You may have heard that you should replace your seeds after two to three years. If you play your cards right and store them properly, you won't need to buy new seeds. You'll be able to use those same seeds for years to come.

Seeds need three things in order to grow: light, heat (or at least warmth), and moisture. The three factors that ensure successful germination are the same factors that will cause seeds to lose viability during storage. By keeping your seeds in the sun, storing them in a hot attic, or laying the packets down on wet soil, you will send your seeds to an early grave. Conversely, if you keep your seeds cool, dark, and dry, they will perform year after year with relative consistency.

So where is a cool, dark, and dry place in your home? Maybe it's a closet or a well-insulated garage. Believe it or not, your refrigerator is the best place to store seeds. But let's not just throw packets in there willy-nilly. There's a method to all of this. Start with a jar that has a lid. Ideally, it should be a jar that you can fit your hand inside. If nothing in your house fits that description, try a plastic or glass container with a tight-fitting lid.

Now scavenge your closet and pantry for a few desiccant packets—you know, those white pouches that come inside packaging when you buy vitamins, shoes, or stereo equipment. They absorb moisture and are perfect for your new seed jar. Toss them in the bottom and insert your seed packets. Close the lid and store the jar in the fridge. That's it.

Wherever you choose to store your seeds, start with lidded seed jars.

GARDENING TIP:
GERMINATION TEST

Do you know where your seeds have been? Out baking in the sun?
Taking a dip in the fountain? A germination test is one sure way to know
whether your seeds are past their prime. Lay a paper towel on a flat
surface and put ten seeds in a straight line across the center, about half
an inch or so (1–2cm) apart. Fold the paper towel up around the seeds,
keeping it flat, and then run it under a stream of water to dampen it.
Place the whole thing in a plastic bag. Seal the bag and place it on top of
your refrigerator, out of direct light. Check back to make sure the paper
towel stays wet.

Seed packets will indicate "days to germination," so mark your
calendar and check for sprouts when time is up. If seven out of ten
seeds germinated, you're in pretty good shape. If five out of ten seeds
germinated, that's a 50 percent germination ratio, so double up on the
number of seeds you plant in each hole. If fewer than 50 percent of the
seeds sprout, scatter the remainder of the packet in a fit of passion or
swap them for newer seeds.

The paper towel and seeds are run under water before being placed in a bag.

TRUSTED SEED COMPANIES

All seed companies listed here have signed the Safe Seed Pledge. Some offer organic seed; others sell untreated seed. All sell heirlooms and open-pollinated seed, with some carrying hybrids as well. Rest assured that none of these companies sell GMO seed. In the political landscape of seed companies, some are at risk of going out of business. See *gardenerd.com/links* for updated and additional information on trusted resources.

SEED COMPANY	CONTACT INFO	NOTES
Baker Creek Heirloom Seeds	rareseeds.com	The mother of heirloom seed catalogs
Botanical Interests	botanicalinterests.com	Family-owned; heirloom and open-pollinated seed; some organic, all untreated
Franchi Seeds/Seeds from Italy	growitalian.com	Traditional Italian varieties; heirloom and open-pollinated vegetables; herbs and flowers
High Mowing Organic Seeds	highmowingseeds.com	Certified organic since 1996
Home Town Seeds	hometownseeds.com	Small family business specializing in survival seed collections
Irish Eyes Garden Seeds	irisheyesgardenseeds.com	Organic seed potatoes, garlic, and vegetable seeds
Johnny's Selected Seeds	johnnyseeds.com	Geared toward farmers with hybrid, heirloom, and open-pollinated varieties; large selection of garden supplies
John Scheepers Kitchen Garden Seeds	kitchengardenseeds.com	In business since 1908
The Living Seed Company	landrethseed.com	Heirloom and open-pollinated seed collections
Native Seeds/SEARCH	nativeseeds.org	Specializes in arid environments and preserving seeds from native cultures in the American Southwest and northwestern Mexico

SEED COMPANY	CONTACT INFO	NOTES
Peaceful Valley Farm & Garden Supply	groworganic.com	Seeds and supplies for farmers and home gardeners
Pinetree Garden Seeds	superseeds.com	Heirloom, open-pollinated, and hybrid seeds; garden and homesteading supplies
Renee's Garden	reneesgarden.com	Carefully curated seed collections and interesting varieties
Seed Savers Exchange	seedsavers.org	Heirloom seeds collected from thousands of members
Seeds of Change	seedsofchange.com	Certified organic seeds, heirlooms, and open-pollinated; some hybrids
Southern Exposure Seed Exchange	southernexposure.com	Strives to preserve seed varieties
Sow True Seed	sowtrueseed.com	Aims to preserve heritage seeds for generations to come
Territorial Seed Company	territorialseed.com	Some open-pollinated and heirloom varieties; some organic seeds and starts
Turtle Tree Biodynamic Seed Initiative	turtletreeseed.org	Biodynamic open-pollinated vegetable and flower seeds
Victory Seed Company	victoryseeds.com	Heirloom seeds; will print custom seed packets for your events
Wood Prairie Family Farm	woodprairie.com	Organic seed potatoes and gifts

GREAT HEIRLOOM/OPEN-POLLINATED SEEDS TO TRY

These are just a few tempting varieties to start you on your way into the world of heirlooms. There are hundreds more than can fit on a page, but these suggestions are fun to grow and interesting to look at while gardening.

FRUIT/VEGETABLE/HERB	VARIETY
Basil	Genovese, Big Leaf, Lettuce Leaf, Opal
Bean, Bush	Dragon Tongue, Roc d'Or Yellow Wax, Maxibel, Black Coco (dry)
Bean, Pole	Christmas Lima, Romano, Cannellini (runner), Scarlet Runner
Beet	Chioggia, Golden, Bull's Blood (for greens too)
Broccoli	Thompson Sprouting, Romanesco, Calabrese, Di Cicco, Early Purple Sprouting
Brussels Sprout	Rubine, Seven Hills
Cabbage	Vertus Savoy, Brunswick, Violaceo di Verona
Carrot	Scarlet Nantes, Cosmic Purple, Yellowstone, Tonda di Parigi
Cauliflower	All the Year Round, Snow's Overwintering, Purple of Sicily
Celery	Utah Tall, Chinese Pink
Chard	Golden, Bright Lights, Fordhook Giant
Collard Greens	Vates, Champion
Corn	Stowell's Evergreen, Japanese Hulless (popping), Blue Hopi (flour)
Cucumber	Mexican Sour Gherkin, Lemon, Armenian, Early Russian
Eggplant	Black Beauty, Listada De Gandia, Rose Bianca
Garlic	Kettle River Giant, Spanish Roja, Inchelium Red
Kale	True Siberian, Lacinato, Red Russian, Vates Blue, Scarlet, Tronchuda Beira
Kohlrabi	Early Purple Vienna, Early White

FRUIT/VEGETABLE/HERB	VARIETY
Leek	King Richard, Scotland, Giant Musselburgh
Lettuce	Rouge d'Hiver, Reine des Glaces, Forellenschluss, Four Seasons, Black Seeded Simpson, Red Oak
Melon	Sharlyn, Hale's Best, Rugoso di Cosenza, Golden Honeymoon
Mustard Greens	Osaka Purple, Mizuna, Tatsoi
Onion	White Lisbon (bunching), Rossa di Milano (red), Texas Early Grano, Red Creole
Parsnip	Turga, Hollow Crown
Pea	Oregon Sugar Snow Pea, Sugar Snap Peas, Alaska (shelling), Green Arrow (shelling)
Pepper	Jimmy Nardello's (sweet), Corno di Toro (sweet), Ancho (hot), Purple Tiger (hot), Fish (hot)
Potato	Cranberry Red, Rose Finn Apple, Russian Banana, All Blue
Pumpkin	Cinderella, Howden, Musquee de Provence, Sugar Baby
Radish	Purple Plum, Watermelon, French Breakfast, Helios, Japanese Minowase
Spinach	Winter Giant, Viroflay, Bloomsdale
Squash, Summer	Cocozelle Zucchini, Bennings Green Tint Patty Pan, Ronde de Nice Zucchini
Squash, Winter	Delicata, Watham Butternut, Table Gold Acorn, Lakota
Tomato	Stupice, Black Cherry, Old German, Great White, Missouri Pink, Green Zebra, Yellow Pear, Garden Peach, Ispolin, Orange Oxheart, Jaune Flamme
Turnip	Purple Top
Watermelon	Moon and Stars, Crimson Sweet, Sugar Baby, Orangeglo

Double digging starts with a 12" (30.5cm) deep trench.

Double Digging

Double digging is often thought of as backbreaking work, and it can be. It is the practice of conditioning the soil to a depth of 24" (61cm) using compost, a shovel, and a digging fork. It is highly recommended to improve clay soils when establishing new garden beds. Whether to continue double digging each year is a point of debate.

- To begin double digging, mark out the planting area. It could be 4' (1.2m) wide and 25' (7.5m) long, or any variation you desire. GROW BIOINTENSIVE, which we talked about in Chapter 5, works with beds that are 100 sq ft (30.5 sq m), so 4' x 25' (1.2 x 7.5m) is ideal if you plan to implement that method.
- Put down a 1" (2.5cm) layer of compost across the entire surface of the bed.
- Starting at one end of the bed, use the shovel to dig a 12" x 12" (30.5 x 30.5cm) trench. Move the soil from that trench into a bucket for later use.
- Optional (use if you have very heavy/clay soil): Add another 1" (2.5cm) of compost to the bottom of the trench.
- Use the digging fork to loosen the soil at the bottom of the trench to a depth of 12" (30.5cm), working the compost (if using) into the cracks as you do. Congrats! You've finished your first trench.
- Dig a second trench, removing the next 12" (30.5cm) of soil. Dump that soil into the first trench.
- Continue adding compost (if needed) and loosening the lower 12" (30.5cm). Repeat the process with each trench.
- When you get to the end of your bed, fill the last trench with the bucket of soil from your first trench. Celebrate with a hot soak afterward.

Start a Compost Bin

A compost bin can be any structure that holds garden biomass (use this term instead of waste, because you're not wasting anything). A compost bin can be a cylinder of hardware cloth, an old trash can with the bottom removed and holes punched in the sides, or an official store-bought compost bin. You don't even need a bin, per se, to store your compost. You can make a pile in your backyard and let it cook. The important thing is to start using your own garden biomass to give back to your garden. Here are a few guidelines for creating a viable composting system.

- **Size:** The ideal minimum size for a compost bin is 3' x 3' x 3' (0.9 x 0.9 x 0.9m). That is the magic size at which organic mass begins to generate and hold heat.
- **Space:** Allow enough space for your compost bin or pile, plus enough space right next to it for another pile. Why? At some point you will want to "turn" the pile (to aerate it and expose new surface area to all of those microbes that will continue to break down the organic matter, which makes the pile heat up again), so ideally you can use that space next to your compost pile to flip a pile from one side to the other without exerting much effort.
- **Browns and greens:** Composting is a chemical reaction between carbon (usually brown-colored biomass) and nitrogen (often, but not always, green-colored biomass). Carbon-rich materials like dried leaves, wood chips, dead corn stalks, wheat chaff, and cardboard are combined with nitrogen-rich materials like kitchen scraps, coffee grounds, grass clippings, cover crops (such as fava beans, alfalfa, and bell beans), and garden trimmings to start the process. See page 232 for an expanded list of browns and greens.

At Gardenerd HQ, we use a three-bin system to turn compost into gardener's gold from start to finish.

- **Other ingredients:**
  Compost requires
  moisture in order to
  break down brown and
  green biomass. Water
  is a key ingredient. In
  climates with regular
  rainfall, you may never
  need to water your
  compost pile once it's
  built. In fact, some
  gardeners have to cover
  their compost piles with
  tarps to keep them from
  getting too wet (excess
  moisture promotes
  anaerobic bacteria—
  the kind that stink). In
  dry climates, though,

Build this active batch thermal compost pile by adding all the ingredients at once and using plenty of water.

  you will need to water your pile regularly. Start by thoroughly watering each layer of the pile as you build it. If you use alfalfa or straw, it will take a lot of water to wet the material completely. Be patient and don't be afraid to use plenty of water. According to Alane O'Rielly Weber, a certified Soil Foodweb advisor at Botanical Arts in San Mateo, California, you should be able to squeeze a drop of water out of a handful of biomass. If not, it's not wet enough. A helpful tip to use as a guideline for moisture is that your pile should be wet like a wrung-out sponge. Water begins the process of biodegradation and invites beneficial microbes to feast upon the decaying matter, so it's a really important ingredient in your pile.

- **Soil:** Soil is another key ingredient, and it is often omitted from many composting guides. You don't need to buy those silly boxes of "compost starter"—use soil instead! Healthy soil inoculates your compost pile with fungi, bacteria, and microorganisms, which go to work to break down organic matter, to aerate the pile as they crawl through, and to digest material. The result is high-powered, high-vitality compost that improves your soil with every application.

- **Layers:** Composting guides vary and will tell you that the ratio of brown material to green material ranges anywhere between one part brown and two parts green to five parts brown and one part green. It can get confusing. Keep it simple. Use depth instead of parts or volume measurements. Put down a 2"–3" (5–7.5cm) layer of browns, then a 2"–3" (5–7.5cm) layer of greens, and then a shovelful of soil, and water it in. Repeat this process until you have used up your ingredients.

Gardenerd Alert: Active Batch Thermal Composting

If you want to get more technical and build an amazing compost pile, try this method for active batch thermal composting. Wait a minute. What the heck does that mean?

- **Active**—You are turning the pile and monitoring temperatures.
- **Batch**—You are building the whole pile all at once rather than adding materials over time.
- **Thermal**—It gets hot, up to 160°F (71°C), with the right materials.
- **Composting**—You are breaking down garden biomass into "black gold."

Here's the method: Figure out how much material your compost bin will hold in gallons (liters). Next, gather your browns and greens in 5 gallon (19L) buckets using the following ratio that Dr. Ingham recommends for beneficial bacterial-dominated compost, which is great for vegetable gardens:

- 35% high-carbon/brown materials like wood chips, sawdust, or dried leaves
- 45% nitrogen/green materials like chipped tree and garden trimmings, coffee grounds, or grass clippings
- 20% high-nitrogen biomass like alfalfa, legume cover crops (such as fava beans), or manures. These high-nitrogen materials kick up the heat quickly and provide food for the bacteria to feast upon.

Note: If you have powdery mildew or other fungal imbalances in your garden, swap the percentages in this list for carbon and nitrogen ingredients for a more fungal-dominant compost. It will help increase fungal diversity to restore balance to garden soils.

Multiply the number of gallons or liters that your compost bin holds by each percentage. That will tell you how many gallons or liters of each type of biomass you will need. Then divide each number by 5, if you are using 5 gallon buckets (or 19, if you are using 19L buckets), and that will tell you how many buckets of each material you will need. For example: if you have a 50 gallon (189L) compost bin, you will need 17.5 gallons (66L), or 3.5 buckets of browns; 22.5 gallons (85L), or 4.5 buckets of greens; and 10 gallons (38L), or 2 buckets, of high-nitrogen/legume/manure materials.

GARDENING TIP:
KEEPING CRITTERS AWAY FROM COMPOST

Always end your composting layers with brown material on top. It keeps away fruit flies, odors, and the vermin who love odors. To add more kitchen waste, pull back the top layer of browns, add your scraps, and then redistribute the brown material on top.

With active batch thermal composting, you don't have to use layers because you are building the pile all at once. You do need to mix the materials together as you put them in the bin, though, and water the pile the entire time. Check the temperatures between 18 and 24 hours after building the pile, and it should be hot. When it gets to 150°F–160°F (65.5°C–71°C), it's time to turn the pile. Each time the pile is turned, it will heat up again (remember, new surface area will be exposed, giving microbes more food to consume). Turn the pile after temperatures peak, again watering thoroughly throughout the process. Repeat turning and watering at least one more time. Eventually the pile will cool down, and, within three to four months, you will have microbe-rich compost for your garden.

If you don't have enough material to build a pile all at once, that's OK. Building a pile over time is still considered composting—cold composting. Your pile will just take longer to process and won't get as hot as active-batch piles do.

BROWNS AND GREENS FOR YOUR COMPOST BIN

BROWNS (MATURE BIOMASS/CARBON)	GREENS (IMMATURE BIOMASS/NITROGEN)

Dried garden plants:
    Corn stalks
    Grain stalks and chaff
    Squash vines
	Green garden plants:
	    Spent flowers
	    Spent vegetable plants (no seeds)
	    Grass clippings (untreated)
	    Weeds (no seeds)

Dried tree leaves	Kitchen scraps (no meat, dairy, fats)
Dried straw/hay	Coffee grounds
Sawdust	Tea leaves
Wood chips	Your hair
Paper egg cartons	Your pet's hair
Cardboards	Your chicken's feathers
Shredded papers	Animal manures (not from dogs or cats—pathogen risk)
Office papers (no metallic inks)	Fresh alfalfa
Junk mail (no glossy pages)	Fresh cover crops—fava beans, clover, vetch, oats, and so on
Used tissues	Hedge trimmings
Used paper towels (use unbleached products)	
Tea bags (avoid "silk" tea bags, which are plastic)	
Coffee filters (unbleached)	
Fabric and lint from natural fibers	

Be sure to add brown ingredients after adding soggy kitchen scraps.

Start a Worm Bin

If you don't have enough room in your garden for a compost bin, consider starting a worm bin to reduce waste and provide high-powered fertilizer for your plants. Worm castings contain concentrated nutrition for plants as well as microbes and chitinase (see Chapter 3 for more details).

Worm bins come in all shapes and sizes. Prices range from a few dollars for a basic plastic tub to more than 100 dollars for an easy-to-use upward-migrating system. If you are just getting started and don't want to spend a lot of money, start with a single-chamber plastic bin.

It's easiest to start with a heavy-duty plastic storage bin that is around 20"–24" (51–61cm) long, about 16" (40.5cm) wide, and 8"–12" (20–30.5cm) tall. Your container should have a lid that snaps on and completely covers the bin. This will prevent water from dripping into the bin during wet weather. Water in the bin leads to drowning accidents. Worms rarely survive such adventures, so keep a lid on it and all will be well.

Your bin requires air holes. Some gardeners prefer to drill ½"–1" (1.25–2.5cm) holes with a paddle bit along the top edge of the container walls (see photo on opposite page), while others like to drill tiny holes (less than ¼" [0.5cm]) along the bottom. Holes on the bottom may allow worms to escape, but they allow leachate, or worm tea, to drain away. If you choose to drill holes in the bottom, stack the worm bin inside a second bin without holes in order to catch the leachate. This will prevent drowning accidents as well.

To make bedding for a single-chamber worm bin, use shredded newspaper, shredded office paper or cardboard, or coir. Many worm-bin kits come with a coir brick. Soak the brick until it expands and absorbs water, and then layer it on the bottom of the bin. Some gardeners like to soak shredded newspaper in water, while others soak fist-sized cardboard pieces instead and mix them with dry, shredded newspaper. Mix shredded paper with shredded newspaper (torn into long strips) to keep the texture of the bedding consistent throughout. Put down a layer of bedding several inches (7–8cm) thick for your worms.

Once you have installed your bedding, it's time for food scraps. Lift up some bedding from one corner of the bin and place some kitchen scraps. Worms like most foods, but there are a few guidelines: no onions, no citrus, no meat, no dairy. Leave out oily foods, and cut up your scraps as small as you can. Worms have to wait for food to begin decomposing before they can eat it. The smaller food scraps are, the quicker they will break down.

Cover the food scraps with the bedding you pulled away, and then cover the entire surface of the bedding with a moist sheet of newspaper. Put the lid on and check regularly, adding food scraps to a different corner each time.

Upward-migrating worm bins, sometimes called worm condos, are fancier domiciles for your worms. There are usually two or three trays that stack on top of each other. The lowest tray is the oldest, and the newest tray is on top with a lid. Each worm bin manufacturer will have specific instructions for preparing the bedding—some use sheets of cardboard on the bottom, others use coir, still others use shredded newspaper with cardboard on top.

When you get one of these bins, start by preparing one tray with food scraps and bedding. As the worms consume the scraps and the tray fills with castings,

You can use a plastic bin with holes drilled across the top. Note the holes at the top edge of the blue bin.

you simply add another tray with food scraps and bedding above it. The worms will migrate up to the next layer, leaving your bottom tray virtually worm-free and ready for harvesting. This feature gives upward-migrating bins an advantage over single-chamber bins.

In a single-chamber bin, when you want to harvest worm castings, you can do one of two things:

1. Move the entire contents of the bedding over to one half of the bin. Add a thick layer of new bedding and some food scraps to the cleared side and wait about two weeks for the worms to migrate to the new area before harvesting the castings from the old side.

2. If you don't have the patience for this technique, dump the entire contents of the bin onto a tarp and make little piles of castings. Worms hate light, so they will burrow to the bottom of each pile. Wear a headlamp to intensify the light, but work in a shady spot out of direct sunlight. Scoop castings off the top of each pile until you have separated the worms from your castings. You will need to combine piles after a while. Return the clump of worms to the bin and deliver the castings to your garden.

A word about storage: shade! Worms hate light and heat. They will die or leave home if you give them inhospitable living conditions. Keep the bin in full shade or in a garage.

Build a Swarm Box for Bees

If you want to dive into urban beekeeping or invite bees into your ecosystem, start by attracting a swarm to your garden. It's not as scary as it sounds. You can order bees by mail, but it's expensive. It's actually better to attract a swarm that may be passing through or one that frequents your yard already. When a swarm is looking for a new home, the bees are at the least aggressive stage in life because they don't have a home or offspring to protect. A swarm box provides a temporary habitat (instead of inside your wall or water-meter box) in which bees can congregate. Once you've collected a swarm in the box, you (or, better yet, a local beekeeper) can transfer the colony to a proper hive that will live on your property.

HoneyLove (*HoneyLove.org*), a nonprofit urban beekeeping organization in Los Angeles, California, is on a mission to educate residents about keeping bees. HoneyLove was instrumental in the effort to legalize beekeeping in Los Angeles and spends countless hours rescuing bees from "unsupported" locations. If a homeowner finds a swarm living in his or her walls, HoneyLove is one of many organizations that will come and remove the colony without killing the bees. The founders of HoneyLove strive to find a home for the bees with a farmer or homeowner in an area where beekeeping is legal.

Rob McFarland of HoneyLove explains that "swarming happens when a thriving colony of bees has outgrown its home. The existing queen and 60 percent of the worker bees exit the hive in search of a new dark, hollow space to colonize, leaving the remaining bees with all the essentials to build the colony back up—honey, pollen, brood (baby bees), and a virgin queen." Swarm boxes can be made from a plethora of materials, including untreated wood (no particle board, please), cardboard boxes, and even wicker baskets. The bees are looking for a hollow cavity with a capacity of between 8 and 10½ gallons (30 and 40L), which equates to a box about 10" (25cm) high x 20" (51cm) wide x 10" (25cm) deep. Be sure to include a small access hole (about 1¼" [3cm] in diameter) on one side of the box, near the bottom. You'll also need a way to cover the hole once bees inhabit the box. You'll screw on rather than nail on the top of the box to make it easier to open the container when it's full of bees.

Build a swarm box to attract a bee colony to your yard.

A swarm of bees hangs from a tree branch and is easy to capture while they are in this, their most docile state.

Some sources suggest hanging foundationless frames inside the box. These are either strips of wood that sit along the top, inside the box (usually coated with a narrow line of beeswax to encourage bees to build a comb there), or wood frames that do not contain a starter sheet of beeswax. The box shown on the opposite page doesn't use frames or strips.

Indigenous communities have made swarm boxes out of wicker baskets (such as small office-sized wastebaskets), each covered securely with a sheet of plywood on top. These baskets, as well as the more formal wooden boxes, can be attached to trees for awaiting bees. To do so, nail a flat piece of wood to the back of the swarm box that extends above the box for several inches (7 or 8cm). Drill a ½" (1.25cm) hole in the extension and hang it on a tree from a nail. You can also secure it on a thick branch. Either way, you will want to make it easy to remove the box when it is full of bees.

There are two other key ingredients in the swarm box: a cotton swab with a dab of lemongrass oil inside and a nearby source of water. Lemongrass mimics the scent of the queen's pheromones, and bees get thirsty and will go elsewhere unless they have access to water. Check your swarm box weekly for a colony and, when it's been colonized, get help moving the bees to a proper hive box—and then get ready for higher yields in the garden.

Solar Food Dryers

Eben Fodor's book *Solar Food Dryer* is filled with detailed charts on how to capture the sun's energy for preserving food. It has step-by-step instructions to build the most efficient solar food dryer possible. You can, too. Here's how:

1. Get the book. Read it cover to cover (it's just over 100 pages). Fodor's instructions detail the involved process, but should you choose to accept this mission, the results are completely satisfying.

2. You can use recycled materials found in your neighborhood, on Craigslist, and at nearby construction sites (no stealing please, but most companies are willing to give you discards). If you have access to Freecycle (a local recycling forum for discarding and acquiring used stuff), look for additional materials there. Make sure that your materials are safe to be used around food. If you're not sure, start with virgin materials.

Stripping the paint is part of the process of recycling a window.

3. Go to the hardware store to get any parts (mostly screws and brackets) you couldn't find recycled. There is an optional electrical component to the project as well, which allows you to plug in two 200-watt light bulbs at night to keep the process going. It calls for porcelain light sockets (they withstand high temperatures). Many hardware stores in the United States do not carry the size needed for this project, so if you cannot find them in a store, look online for Leviton 9880 medium surface-mount porcelain light sockets. You will also need to locate food-grade screen material, which is not made from vinyl like regular window screening.

4. Put on your math cap. Recalculate the dimensions in Fodor's book to account for your recycled materials. His glass window was 27 ¾" x 30" (70.5 x 76cm). Let's say yours is long and narrow instead: 48" x 15" (122 x 38cm). You will need to adjust

the dimensions for length and width on all related parts and reduce your screen size to 2" (5cm) smaller than your window. Keep in mind that, with narrow windows, the angle of the glass (to capture the sun's rays) changes.

5. Cut all materials with a table saw. Get help from a carpenter friend or family member if you are clumsy or fear losing a finger. Always wear protective goggles and use a push stick. **Note:** Don't use plywood for legs or rear braces; use solid wood.

6. Assemble your solar food dryer. Start with the ends that hold the legs and interior rails for holding drying trays and a metal absorber plate.

   Connect the ends with the cross pieces to create a standing frame. Add the bottom panel to hold the frame square. This may require another set of hands to hold it in place while drilling in screws.

7. Install the electrical backup lighting (if using) to ensure continued drying overnight and when temperatures drop due to clouds or fog. This is highly recommended if you live in an area with coastal marine-layer conditions. The lighting elements can keep the unit between 90°F and 120°F (32°C and 49°C) overnight, depending on wattage.

These are the end pieces of the solar food dryer.

Here, we connect the end pieces with front and back frames.

With the unit almost completely assembled, the electrical wiring goes in before installation can continue.

8. Cut, shape, paint, and install the absorber plate. Standard thin sheet metal works great for this project. It cuts easily with tin snips. Making the proper folds in the design can be a little challenging, but if you enlist the help of a friend, it will be much easier to bend sheet metal in a specific place without the use of heavy machinery (hint: use the edge of a piece of wood and four hands).

Attaching the metal absorber plate.

Fodor's book says to paint the sheet metal with high-temperature stove paint. One glance at the label on that paint can may make you shy away from having stove paint anywhere near your food. It off-gasses like mad for a few days, so leave the painted absorber plate out in the sun as long as possible before assembling. As an alternative, you could opt for a nontoxic metal paint. DecoArt No-Prep Metal Paint works like a charm, and it is available online and at some craft stores.

9. Finish the assembly. This unit uses natural convection, with screened openings on the bottom and top to facilitate airflow. The top has a vent door to regulate airflow and temperature. The vents are covered with regular screen material to keep insects out. Install the access door and vents.

Attaching the door and vent.

10. Now, for the window. The book uses just the glass part, but if your dimensions include the frame, don't remove it. Attach the window to the dryer and bracket it into place. Use a vise to bend the brackets as needed.

11. Add a thermometer for tracking temperatures (requires a small hole in the side of the unit) and your food-safe screens, and start dehydrating!

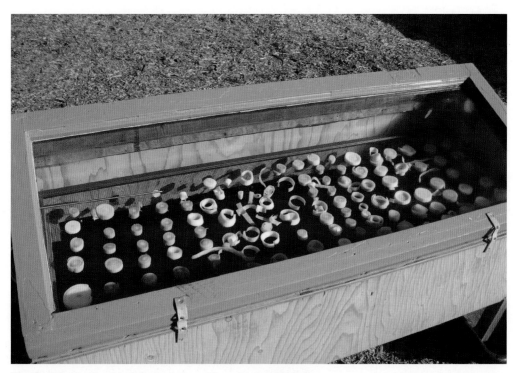

The finished solar food dryer is in action, drying leeks.

The total cost for making the unit featured here was $118.84, including new screening, sheet metal, hardware, electrical wiring and fixtures, and one small hole in the hand (wayward drill). Salvaged materials included the window, screen, wood, some hardware, staples, reflective tape, and elbow grease. Relatively speaking, you can spend $300 or more on a fancy high-powered electric dryer, but you still have to plug it in. Given that it is nearly impossible to find solar food dryers for sale, it makes this machine priceless, not to mention that the satisfaction of building something with your own hands is beyond joyful.

A cheese-making thermometer works perfectly for this task.

Be sure to use a food-safe screen.

Bibliography and Resources

As with the list of trusted seed companies, these resources are bound to change. Visit *gardenerd.com* for up-to-date recommendations.

Books and Articles

Allen, Will, Diana Balmori, and Fritz Haeg. *Edible Estates: Attack on the Front Lawn,* second edition. Pasadena, CA: Metropolis Books, 2010.

Anderson, Arthur B., and Charles B. Wilke. "Solvent Seasoning of Redwood," Oregon State University, 1965.

Bartholomew, Mel. *All New Square Foot Gardening.* Minneapolis, MN: Cool Springs Press, 2006.

Bell, Mary T. *Mary Bell's Complete Dehydrator Cookbook.* New York: William Morrow, 1994.

Bradley, Fern Marshall, editor. *Rodale's Garden Answers.* Emmaus, PA: Rodale Press, 1995.

Bradley, Fern Marshall, Barbara W. Ellis, and Deborah L. Martin. *The Organic Gardener's Handbook of Natural Pest and Disease Control.* Emmaus, PA: Rodale Books, 2010.

Carpenter-Boggs, L., J.P. Reganold, and A. C. Kennedy. "Effects of Biodynamic Preparations on Compost Development." *Biological Agriculture and Horticulture,* vol. 17 (2000), 313-318.

Creasy, Rosalind. *Edible Landscaping.* San Francisco, CA: Sierra Club Books, 2010.

Evans, Erv. "Nutrient Content of Natural Materials," North Carolina State University, 2000.

Fodor, Eben. *The Solar Food Dryer: How to Make and Use Your Own Low-Cost, High-Performance, Sun-Powered Food Dehydrator.* Gabriola Island, Canada: New Society Publishers, 2006.

Gardeners and Farmers of Centre Terre Vivante. *Preserving Food without Freezing or Canning.* White River Junction, VT: Chelsea Green Publishing, 2007.

Hamilton, Geoff. *Organic Gardening,* second edition. New York: DK Publishing, 2011.

Hemenway, Toby. *Gaia's Garden: A Guide to Homescale Permaculture,* second edition. White River Junction, VT: Chelsea Green Publishing, 2009.

Ingham, Dr. Elaine. *Soil Biology Primer.* Soil and Water Conservation Society, in cooperation with the USDA Natural Resources Conservation Service, 2000.

Jeavons, John. *How to Grow More Vegetables,* eighth edition. New York: Ten Speed Press, 2012.

Kingry, Judy and Lauren Devine. *Ball Complete Book of Home Preserving.* Toronto, Canada: Robert Rose, 2006.

Kiser, Mark, and Selena Kiser. "A Decade of Bathouse Discovery," *The Bat House Researcher,* vol. 12, no. 1 (2004).

Kourik, Robert. *Drip Irrigation for Every Landscape and All Climates*, second edition. Occidental, CA: Metamorphic Press, 2009.

———. *Roots Demystified*. Occidental, CA: Metamorphic Press, 2007.

Lowenfels, Jeff, and Wayne Lewis. *Teaming with Microbes*. Portland, OR: Timber Press, 2011.

Mollison, Bill. *Introduction to Permaculture*. Berkeley, CA: Ten Speed Press, 1997.

Nancarrow, Loren, and Janet Hogan Taylor. *The Worm Book*. Berkeley, CA: Ten Speed Press, 1998.

Pfeiffer, Ehrenfried. *Pfeiffer's Introduction to Biodynamics*. Edinburgh, Scotland: Floris Books, 2011.

Pleasant, Barbara. "Know When to Plant What: Find Your Average Last Spring Frost Date," *Mother Earth News*, July 30, 2008.

Reynolds, Susan. "Drying Vegetables," University of Florida Cooperative Extension Service Institute of Food and Agricultural Services, 1994.

Rich, Deborah K. "The Case Against Synthetic Fertilizers," SanFranciscoGate.com, January 14, 2006.

Riotte, Louise. *Carrots Love Tomatoes*. North Adams, MA: Storey Publishing, 1998.

Rodale Institute, "Collecting, Keeping Wild Honeybees Boosts Coffee Yield, Adds New Layer of Agroecological Stability," Cheryl Miller, Sustainable Harvest International, March 31, 2010.

Sheikh, Bahman. "White Paper on Gray Water," WateReuse Association, Water Environment Federation, and American Water Works Association, 2010.

Stout, Ruth. "Have a Garden without an Aching Back." *Mother Earth News Magazine*, February/March, 2004.

_____. "How to Grow Without Digging." *Organic Gardening Magazine*, vol. 58.1, p.49.

Walliser, Jessica. *Plant Partners*. North Adams, MA: Storey Publishing, 2020.

Waskom, R. M., T. Bauder, J. G. Davis, and A. A. Andales, "Diagnosing Saline and Sodic Soil Problems," Fact sheet number 0.521, Colorado State University Extension, July 2003.

Websites and Organizations

American Community Garden Association: *communitygarden.org*

Backwards Beekeeping: *backwardsbeekeepers.com*

The Bug Guide: *bugguide.net*

Slow Food: *slowfood.com*

Glossary

annual—A plant that completes its life cycle in one season or year. It dies when it's finished growing and is replaced the following year. Sweet basil is an annual. When an annual dies at the end of the season, it's not your fault; it's what nature intended.

axil—The upper angle between the leaf and stem of a plant.

berm beds—Berms are a raised planting area, usually created by mounding soil up. Berm beds, then, are beds planted on berms.

biodynamics—The term used for a holistic approach to agriculture that emphasizes natural methods of growing and fertilizing and stays away from artificial pesticides and soil additives. Biodynamic gardening tries to integrate all aspects of the ecosystem in the garden, including plants, animals, and irrigation. It was first proposed by Rudolf Steiner in the 1920s.

biomass—Biological material from living (or recently living) organisms. For the purposes of this book, biomass includes mature (dried/dead carbon-rich) materials, such as fallen leaves, and immature (living nitrogen-rich) materials, such as green garden waste and kitchen scraps.

bolt to seed—When a plant is stressed by hot weather or not enough water, or is at the end of its life cycle, it begins to elongate, sending up a flower stalk from the center of the plant. A seedhead forms at the top—a last gasp to produce offspring before dying. Most plants lose flavor or become tough and bitter when this occurs. Bolting to seed indicates that it's time to pull out the plant and compost it.

coir—A fiber taken from coconut husks. It's used in many products; in gardening, it can be used as a substitute for peat moss.

compost tea—A water solution that contains nutrients from compost as well as a multitude of beneficial soil microbes. Essentially, it concentrates the biological benefits of compost. You can find many recipes and equipment online for brewing compost tea properly.

direct-seeding—The process of sowing seeds in the ground exactly where you want them to mature. Plants that have trouble germinating or are sensitive to cold weather prefer to be started indoors in seed trays. Many crops, however, can be direct-seeded: lettuces, greens, root crops, and nonwoody herbs are the easiest.

earthbags—Polypropylene bags that are filled with soil and used as building material. Some architects refer to this technique as superadobe because they fill the bags with adobe, or heavy clay soil. The popularity of using earthbags is on the rise.

emitters—Simply put, the openings in drip tubing where water comes out. There are different types of emitters: inline emitters are built into the tubing, and online emitters are attached to the outside of tubing. Drip tubing is available with emitters spaced 6", 12", 18", or 24" (15, 30.5, 46, or 61cm) apart.

exudates—The acids, sugars, and enzymes that plants secrete through their roots in the rhizosphere (area surrounding the roots). They can be excreted as a defense mechanism against pathogenic microorganisms in the soil, or they can feed beneficial microbes in the soil food web.

inoculant—A black powder that is used to coat bean and pea seeds before planting. The inoculant introduces rhizobia bacteria into the soil, which allows the legume roots to begin forming nodules for fixing nitrogen. Once soils are populated with these bacteria, you don't need to use inoculants again. If you are planting in a new area each year, though, use inoculants as you sow bean and pea seeds.

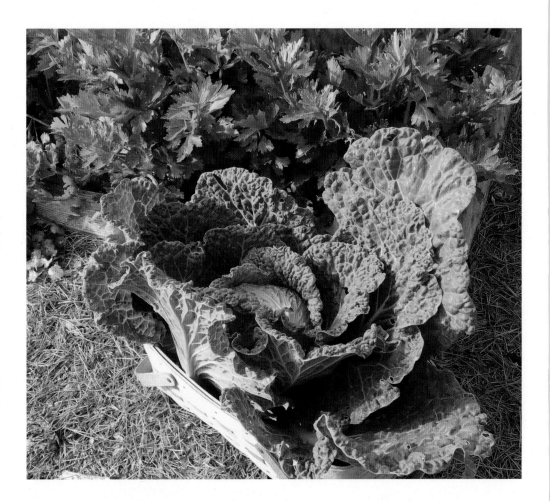

loam—Soil that's made up of more or less equal proportions of sand, silt, and clay. It's the type of soil that is great for gardening and is the goal that every gardener strives for when working amendments into their soil.

monoculture—The method of producing a single kind of crop in a given area for many years. Although big agricultural farms use this technique, it's antithetical to what small farmers and gardeners believe creates biodiversity and healthy soil.

olla—An unglazed jug with a long neck that is buried in the ground, leaving only the jug's open mouth exposed. Gardeners fill ollas with water, which seeps through porous walls into the soil, right where the roots need it.

perennial—A longer-lasting plant that lives longer than a year. A tree is a perennial.

permaculture—A set of principles or design tools created by Bill Mollison and David Holmgren that are used to develop ecological systems. These principles are applied to architecture, agriculture, and self-reliance to work in concert with nature and restore balance to damaged landscapes.

potting soil—As mentioned earlier, there's no actual soil in potting soil. Instead, it contains decomposed organic matter and perlite, which helps with drainage. Potting soil also often contains peat moss or coir.

"three sisters" garden—A First Nations tradition of interplanting beans, corn, and winter squash together. The Iroquois understood that these three plants were beneficial companions. Beans use the corn as a trellis, corn benefits from nitrogen-fixing beans, and squash plants provide a living mulch with their broad leaves. Corn is planted first, then beans are planted next to each corn stalk, and then squash is planted around the perimeter of the planted area to provide shade for the root systems.

tilth—A gardening term used to describe soil that has the right structure and nutrients to grow stuff. It's related to the word till, as in "till the soil."

tree collard—A perennial vegetable that is part of the brassica family. It is a bit sweeter than related veggies, such as kale. Tree collard is also unusual in that it grows to be as tall as 11' (3.5m). It is an integral part of GROW BIOINTENSIVE and permaculture gardens as a perennial food source.

unconstructed bed—Another term for these beds is open mound beds. They don't have sides and can be built up to 6" (15cm) or more above ground level with soil and organic matter.

volunteer(ing)—A plant that grows all by itself, from seeds unknown, is a volunteer. If vegetables are left to go to seed in the garden, the likelihood of volunteering is much higher. Some gardeners let cilantro, arugula, and dill go to seed each year in hopes of having an abundant volunteer crop next season. Many times, volunteers grow to be stronger and more prolific than anything planted deliberately. We like to call them "nature's slap in the face."

Index

Note: Page numbers in **bold** indicate herb and vegetable profiles (with specific growing, harvesting, and common problems information). Page numbers in *italics* indicate recipes.

mini-greenhouse (cloche), 221
morning glory, 181
mounded (berm) beds, 32–33
mounded raised beds, 34–35
mustard greens, 58, **119**, 144, *196*, 227. *See also*
brassicas

N

nasturtium, 16, 181
netting, for plant support and pest control,
164–65, 179
nightshades (Solanaceae), 61. *See also specific
plants*
nitrogen (N)
  about: soil nutrients and, 38
  amount of, 47–48
  benefits and sources, 48–49
  compost and, 229, 231, 232
  crop rotation and, 62–63
  in fertilizer, 48–49
  fixing into soil, 46–47
  testing soil for, 43–44
  worm castings for, 52–53
nursery stock
  to avoid, 91
  with flowers/fruit (avoiding), 91
  planting from, 89–92
  proper techniques, 91–92
  selecting, 90–91
  transplant shock and, 92
nutrients, in soil, 38. *See also* nitrogen (N);
phosphorus (P); potassium (K)
nylon plant supports, 164–65

O

onions. *See* green onions
open-pollinated seeds, 93
oregano, **140**, 145, 190, 200–1
organic fertilizer, 48–50
orientation of garden, 17–18
oven dehydration, 190

P

parasitic wasps (Aphelinidae family), 174, 176,
181
parsley, **141**, 144, 181, 187, 191, 200–1
peas, **120–21**, 144. *See also* bean/pea (Fabaceae/
Leguminosae) family; trellises
  blanching/freezing times, 188
  companion planting, 64–65
  cool-season crops and, 57–58
  drying/dehydrating, 189–91
  nitrogen and, 46, 63
  saving seeds, 89
  seeds to try, 227
  sugar snap pea, 143
  Tender Crisp Steamed Veggies with a Kick,
198
peppers, **122–23**, 144
  drying/dehydrating, 189–91
  freezing without blanching, 189
  plant placement, 19–20
  plant/trellis partnerships, 166
  saving seeds, 88
  seeds to try, 227
  storage guidelines, 187
  warm-/hot-season crops and, 59
pest control, 170–83. *See also specific plants*

Photo Credits

All photographs by Christy Wilhelmi unless otherwise indicated.

Leaf graphic, pages 8, 12, 22, 36, 54, 70, 86, 146, 160, 170, 184: DRogatnev/Shutterstock

Photographs and graphic, pages 15, 236, 237: Courtesy of HoneyLove.org

Sidebar border, pages 16, 18, 26, 32, 50, 60, 88, 89, 155, 169, 187, 190, 193, 194, 209, 214, 220, 223, 231: Miloje/Shutterstock

Compass rose graphic, pages 19, 67, 68, 69: StockAppeal/Shutterstock

Food web graphic, page 40: Courtesy of United States Department of Agriculture

Sign background, pages 95, 135: Christopher Elwell/Shutterstock

Romaine lettuce photo, page 143: SP2707/Shutterstock

Shallot photo, page 145: Hasrul Hendrawan/Shutterstock

Raised bed graphic, page 211: Courtesy of Gardenerd

Author photo, page 248: Emily Murphy @passthepistil

The following images are courtesy of Shutterstock:

Alison Hancock, 34

AmyLv, 63

Andrii Zastrozhnov, 134

Anton Starikov, 51

Antonina Potapenko, 31

ArieStudio, 185

Arina P Habich, 71

Beloborod, 129

Bondar Illia, 61

Cattlaya Art, 224–25

Chiyacat, 84

Cornel Constantin, 175 (top)

COULANGES, 175 (bottom left)

Daniela Pelazza, 14

Denis Pogostin, 101, 125

Dolly Marlin J, back cover

domnitsky, 53

Emil Timplaru, 1

encierro,10–11

Esin Deniz, 110

Hans Verburg, 65

HelloRF Zcool, 173

Joanne Dale, 81

Joseph C, 164

Jukov studio, 37

Jurga Jot, 112

Kazakova Maryia, 7, 194

Keith Homan, 205

Luuuusa, 20

memphisslim, 41

Michele Paccione, 56

Miro Vrlik Photography, 250

MNStudio, 255

Monthira, 49

Mrs.Rungnapa akthaisong, 233

My July, 6

Nattika, 191

nblx, 100

nednapa, 80

Norman Chan, 121

Odua Images, 30

rng, 200

rootstock, 165

Simol1407, 214

Simone Hogan, 175 (bottom right)

Singkham, 45

smereka, 98

ThomasPhoto, 21

Tompet, 148

Trieu Tuan, 47

unamarina, 123

Vadym Zaitsev, 179

vermontalm, 180

Vintagepix, 206–7

Vladimir Konstantinov, 193

Whiteaster, 198

wildJune, 41

yarinkamorozova, 149

Zoia Kostina, 132

About the Author

Christy Wilhelmi is owner of Gardenerd, the ultimate resource for garden nerds, where she publishes newsletters, her popular blog, top-ranked podcasts, and YouTube videos. She specializes in small-space, organic-vegetable garden design, consulting, and classes. Between 50 and 70 percent of her family's produce comes from her garden of less than 300 sq ft (28 sq m).

Christy is the author of *Grow Your Own Mini Fruit Garden* (Cool Springs Press, April 2021), *400+ Tips for Organic Gardening Success* (Amazon Digital), and her debut novel *Garden Variety* (William Morrow/Harper Collins, April 2022).